HOW TO BECOME WEALTHY THROUGH REAL ESTATE

ARJUN SINGH

Contents

Contents

Contents

Acknowledgements

Dear readers,

Welcome to this book, your ultimate guide to achieving financial freedom through real estate. I am thrilled to have you join me on this exciting journey towards a life of abundance and independence. Real estate stands as a powerful avenue for building wealth and forging a secure financial future. Throughout the pages of this book, my goal is to equip you with practical strategies, expert insights, and proven techniques that can empower you to navigate the real estate world with confidence.

I understand the challenges that arise when pursuing financial freedom. My mission is to share the knowledge and wisdom I've acquired, helping you unlock the doors to prosperity.

Whether you are a novice investor or someone with prior experience, this book caters to all levels of expertise. From comprehending market dynamics to making sound investment decisions and constructing a profitable portfolio, we will address it all. But financial freedom is not just about making money; it's also about making informed choices and fostering a mindset of abundance. As we journey together, I encourage you to embrace growth, nurture perseverance, and always remember that every step forward, regardless of its size, brings you closer to your dreams.

I extend sincere gratitude to my real estate mentor, **Mr. Amit Sangwan** Sir, from whom I've gained this knowledge. I wish to express my appreciation to my wife, mother, and sister for their unwavering support during the writing of this book. Their encouragement has served as a driving force, and I hope this book adds value to your lives.

To all readers, thank you for investing your time and trust in this book. May the knowledge shared here empower you to embark on a journey towards financial freedom through real estate, leading to a future brimming with possibilities.

Wishing you all the success and prosperity that this journey can offer.
Sincerely,
Arjun Singh

CHAPTER I

Why understanding all aspects of real estate is important.

"Buying real estate is not only the best way but also the quickest and safest way to become wealthy.—Marshall Field "

Real estate holds paramount importance in our lives, encompassing wealth, happiness, and relationships. It represents the largest investment we make. Our parents strive to provide us with the best education, and we work hard to secure a spot in top colleges and attain respectable jobs. Following this, marriage and parenthood come into play. As we progress, the idea of owning a house takes center stage. However, many people postpone this decision, ultimately struggling to buy a home due to soaring inflation and insufficient savings. You might have observed individuals in your social circle who didn't excel academically and now hold average, low-paying jobs in their hometowns. Yet, they or their parents invested in real estate at the opportune time without delay. This prudent choice leaves them better positioned with assets, peace of mind, and regular cash flows. Despite their modest income, their lifestyle and contentment often exceed yours. Conversely, despite your exceptional academic achievements and a lucrative position in a multinational corporation, saving money becomes a challenge. Each month brings unforeseen expenses that hinder your ability to save. Frequent extravagant trips for social media appearances, purchasing a car right after landing a job to maintain an image, partying every weekend, high rent payments, and dabbling in stock market trading with your limited savings for quick riches lead to losses. The long-term stocks you hold fail to perform, and your capital remains stagnant even after several years. Consequently, by the age of 35, homeownership remains a distant dream. It may seem that those who fared worse academically than you are outpacing you in terms of net worth, monthly cash flow, and tranquility. Occasionally, you encounter friends whose parents acquired properties two decades ago, and the appreciation in property values far surpasses what your prestigious IIT or IIM degree can achieve. Nevertheless, do not lose hope. A chance to equal their level of assets within 15-20 years still exists. You can pass on these assets to the next generation, providing support even if your children's careers don't flourish. Investing in real estate during your 20s or 30s yields rewards when you will cross age of 45 having responsibilities such as college fees and wedding expenses for your children. Real estate investments secure your golden years and ensure a stable future for generations to come. Though not characterized by short-term high returns, real estate offers gradual and consistent income along with capital appreciation. You can conquer anxiety and fear regarding your children's education, their employment prospects, their marriages, and your retirement income."I am quoting Goddess Laxmi ji ki arti here "दूरगारपुनरिंजनी, सुखसम्पत्तदिाता।,जो कोई तुम को ध्यावत, ऋद्धि-सिद्धि धिन पाता॥ जसि घर में तुम रहती, सबसद्गुण आता।,सब सम्भव हो जाता, मन नहीं घबराता॥" Which means "Whoever meditates upon you, receives prosperity, happiness and success. In the home where you reside, all virtues manifest. All possibilities become attainable, and the mind remains fearless." It means that whoever have assets and cash flows are happy, prosper and fearless. People used to spend a lot of time researching before buying a Rs. 10,000/- mobile phone. However, when it comes to real estate, they often make decisions based on others' opinions without much thought. Unfortunately, there aren't any good books available in the market that provides knowledge about real estate for middle-class individuals. The few books that are available are either meant for becoming a real estate broker and focus on sales and marketing techniques, or they are autobiographies where authors talk about their own achievements and how they became billionaires. However, the knowledge in those books is often not applicable for normal middle-class people.

CHAPTER II

History of Real Estate in India

"Investing in real estate is smart because property is tangible. People always have, and always will, need shelter. This means it is very unlikely that our need for shelter will ever go away.—Kathy Fettke "

In ancient times, even during the Harappa and Mohenjo-Daro civilizations, real estate existed. The distance of a property from the king's fort would determine its price. The elite and the rich class would reside in higher places, while the poor and lower class would live in low-lying areas. When the British arrived, real estate growth was more pronounced in places where British offices were situated, such as Delhi and Kolkata. The British carefully selected specific cities and locations within them, like Lutyens' Delhi, which experienced exponential growth in value. The areas where the British resided commanded the highest real estate prices, and the value of a real estate property was gauged based on its proximity to these areas where British offices were established. Even in today's times, this concept remains relevant, albeit without the presence of kings. In the modern era, real estate develops around government offices, economic hubs, railway stations, airports, schools, and hospitals. For instance, in large cities, the distance of a property from Special Economic Zones (SEZs) or job-generating centers significantly determines its price. The closer a property is to an SEZ, the higher its value. A general guideline is to seek property within a 30-minute commute from the city center. In ancient times, this 30-minute commute could be traversed on foot, covering approximately 2 km, resulting in a city with an approximate 2 km radius. With the advent of bullock carts and horse-drawn carriages, the 30-minute distance expanded to around 5 km. During the British colonial era, with the introduction of automobiles, the same 30-minute distance equated to a radius of 10 km from the city center. In today's context, you can measure the 30-minute commute from your flat or plot to SEZs, airports, railway stations, government offices, economic hubs, schools, or any upcoming infrastructure development or job creation center. It is crucial to analyze and identify the city's central points or hubs. Utilizing this 30-minute commute from your real estate investment to center of the city as a guiding principle can greatly aid in property selection. While considering the purchase of property, it's essential to observe where the elite or rich class prefers to reside and understand people's residential aspirations. Identifying areas which will be develop as aspiration living areas for rich in the future is important aspect for decision-making process for buying real estate.

CHAPTER III

Investing in Real Estate and Equity

"I will forever believe that buying a home is a great investment. Why? Because you can't live in a stock certificate. You can't live in a mutual fund.—Oprah Winfrey"

In this chapter, our focus is not to determine whether Real Estate or Equity is superior. Instead, we understand the importance of having exposure to both these investment avenues. Both real estate and stock market investments hold substantial roles within an investment portfolio. In the realm of equity, one can analyze historical technical charts of individual stocks or indices to know historical returns. Whereas evaluating returns of a micro-market or specific area in real estate is challenging due to limited data availability. Moreover due to the involvement of cash transactions, finding actual buying and selling prices is tough as registry data often includes only official white money transactions. This is why stories about stocks are more common in newspapers compared to real estate. While stories of real estate appreciation circulate within personal circles, they rarely make public headlines, remaining relatively less prominent than equity. The equity market involves many stakeholders, including government bodies, banks, mutual fund managers, industry experts, corporate owners, and employees. This involvement makes the stakes high in equity market. Due to involvement of too many stake holders, Mutual funds and stocks are promoted everywhere. Everyone want that price of stocks and NIFTY Index should be high as NIFTY is barometer of Economy. However, if you are buying a small plot or flat, only the seller or builder's stakes are involved. That's why equity is promoted more while real estate is not promoted as much. In equity, the probability of profit from individual stocks is often low, and 90% of individuals who engage in short-term trading or investing end up with returns lower than fixed deposit yields. However, this is not the case in real estate. Roughly 95% of real estate investors outperform Fixed Deposit returns. Yet, investing in real estate can be tough due to the generally higher ticket size, potentially putting one's life savings at risk if things go bad that's why suffering is much higher in real estate. That's why people are afraid to invest in real estate. On the other hand, in stocks, you invest a small amount of your savings, and it is also diversified among different stocks, so if one stock incurs losses, your capital does not get wiped out. But the truth is that even if you invest a small amount in equity and get exceptionally good returns, it doesn't make a significant difference in your overall net worth or wealth because a large portion of your capital is still invested in savings, fixed deposits, or real estate. Financial influencers believe in formula-based returns, such as invest Rs. 15,000/- per month for 15 years and get Rs. 1 Cr assuming historical CAGR of 15% but financial influencers forget that past results do not necessarily predict future returns. The older the historical return data, the less likely it'll be successful at forecasting returns in the future. One more idea financial influencers give that if you want to buy house of Rs.1 Cr, you can buy that house by doing SIP of Rs. 15,000/- per month for 15 years assuming 15% CAGR and after 15 years you can buy a house priced Rs. 1 Cr. In this calculation, financial influencers forget to consider inflation and they don't tell you that after 15 years, if property appreciation is considered at 11%, including 8% inflation, the value of the property will be Rs. 5 Cr after 15 years. If you ask any financial influencer about real estate they will simply tell you that if you buy a property of Rs. 1.2 Cr and if you take Rs. 1 Cr loan and Rs. 20 lakhs from your own savings then you have to pay Rs. 1 Cr extra for a loan of 20 years so total amount you have to pay Rs. 2.2 Cr. They will tell you that rental yield is only 2-2.5% and home loan interest is 9% so rental yield is far less than EMI so it is not a financial prudent decision to buy home but they will never tell you that interest rates are decreasing as it was 10.5% in 2012 and now it is 8% and it may decrease further as we are following economy of developed countries so it can be 6% after 10 years. Financial influencers never tell you that your rent will be increasing each year around 8-10% and rents will be double after each 7-8 years and rent will be four to five times of current rents after 20 years' time span. After 20 years when EMI will not be there you will get 25-30% yearly returns on your invested amount. Financial influencers will never tell you about the income tax benefit that you will get per month. They will never tell you that your property will also get appreciated each year at least 7% if you consider only inflation. Financial influencer will never tell you that when you buy under construction property, your own savings is not going at one go but it will go slowly in 4-5 years so you will get time of 4-5 years to complete full payment. Financial influencers will not tell you that you can prepay loan in 8-9 years as your salary will also double in each 8-9 years. Financial influencers will not tell you tell in future, flat size will be smaller. If today you are getting 2 BHK in size of 1200 sqft., it may happen that after 7-8 years you will get 2 BHK of 850-990sqft. at inflated price. Financial influencers will not tell you that loan amount of Rs. 1 Cr today will be like Rs. 25 lakhs loan amount after 20 years considering 9% inflation. The value of the loan decreases gradually year after year due to inflation. The biggest drawback in equity, whether in mutual funds or individual stocks, is that you cannot use leverage for investing. You can use leverage in the Future and Options trading and in Intraday trading, but there your capital can get wiped out very easily. If you have Rs. 10 lakhs today, depending on your loan eligibility you can use leverage to buy an under-construction flat worth Rs. 1 Cr and your returns will be on Rs. 1 Cr. But in equity, if you have Rs. 10 lakhs you can only invest Rs. 10 lakhs and your return will be on Rs. 10 lakhs only. In an under-construction flat, your savings is released in 4 years, so you get leverage of 90-95% instead of 80%. With more leverage, the returns on your invested capital increase. If the price of Rs.1 Cr flat increases by 20%in 3-4 years and you invested Rs. 10 lakhs initially then the appreciation of will be on the Rs. 1 Cr, which is Rs. 20 lakhs. When you have your own home, you will get peace of mind which cannot calculated in excel and in terms of CAGR. A house is like insurance for your family. If you take term insurance you will get amount only after death but if you take house if will take care of your family before and after your death. If you have a home, your social status will increase, as if you have cleared one level up in the game of life. It is advisable to invest both in real estate and equity. If you want to invest in both equity and real estate, one way is to take a loan for real estate property and invests rents in SIP mode in equity. For example, if you take a flat on a loan, initially the EMI is higher than the rent, but after 6-7 years, when the rent of your property becomes higher than the EMI, you can invest the difference between rent and EMI as a monthly SIP in any mutual fund or index fund. The benefits are that first you will get capital appreciation on your property. Second, your rents will be invested in mutual funds so you will get capital appreciation in equity by investing in mutual funds. Third, as yearly rents will increase by 8-10% each year, so your SIP in mutual funds will also increase so it will be like step up mode SIP in mutual funds like each year your SIP amount will increase will by 8-10%. If you don't want to invest in SIP and want to invest only when share market is down, one more strategy is to invest the monthly rents in recurring deposits

(RDs). Whenever there is a mini or major crash in the Stock market (in general, a major crash occurs every 8-10 years, and minor crashes happen every 3-4 years), you can break those monthly RDs and invest the amount in index funds or any low cost good mutual funds. This way, you can get equity at very good valuations, and their risk-reward ratio will be excellent.

CHAPTER IV

You should always be get informed in Real Estate

"There's always opportunity in real estate. It's just a matter of finding that opportunity in the current market.—Samantha DeBianchi"

If you want to buy a property in a particular area and if you don't have budget it does not mean that if you should drop your plan of buying property and completely cut off from that area. Even if your budget does not allow, you should still get informed of that particular area or city like what are the developments going on, name of the builders those are launching projects, rental yields of areas, information regarding upcoming projects, name of builders acquiring big land parcels. You can get these information from various forum like indianrealestateboard, Youtube blogs, daily newspaper, brokers, whtsapp groups, any friends or relative residing in that area. Even if you are not able to buy flat, you should aware of all happenings of that area so that when you have sufficient cash from savings you can invest in that area whenever good opportunity comes. If you adopt this type of strategy you don't need to rely on brokers for getting information and you can directly ask your doubts from them. If you don't have information on that area, you will not able to take decision to buy property when broker shows you the property. You can compare these phenomena with example of buying a stock or mutual fund. Whenever you buy any stock you analyze technical chart history of that particular stock, Industry in which that stock is performing, Historical performance of Index, Fundamental analysis of that stock like 5 years balance sheet and Profit and loss analysis. In the case of Mutual fund you see the performance of that mutual fund like how much alpha is generated by that fund and asset under management and the group to which that fund belong, and expense ratio. All these information you can get just by a click on Zerodha.com and Screener.in but in case of purchasing flat, history of that micro market or area where you are buying a property ,Price movement of that area, Development of that area, Gentry or class that is living in that area, aspirations of people to reside in that area you cannot know completely on internet. You can get some idea of property prices and rent from 99acres and magickbricks but for many areas data is insufficient on internet so you have to physically visit that areas and get information also from youtube, whtsapp and telegram groups.

CHAPTER V

Bottom-up approach for deploying money in Real Estate.

"Real estate is like Jack and the Beanstalk's goose that lays golden eggs. It's something that pays you month after month, whether you are working or not.—Kathy Fettke"

If your sole objective in real estate is pure investment, it is recommended to consider purchasing a small size flat as small size flats often provide higher rental yields. Opting for a 1 BHK fully furnished flat (one-bedroom, hall, and kitchen) flat would be ideal for getting good rentals and if you are not getting 1 BHK you can go for small size 2BHK. Similarly, if you are interested in buying a plot in non-metro city for investment, it is advisable to choose one that is located near outskirts of the city and you have to make sure that the area must be livable in 10-15 years so you can buy that land for investment horizon for at least 10-15 years. If you buy land at heart of the city, it may happen that appreciation will be less because already developed areas tend to have lower percentage-wise appreciation. It's comparable to teaching a child to improve their scores from 30 to 60, which is relatively easier than improving score from 90 to 95, which is more challenging. When you find something available at a lower cost, particularly at the bottom of the pyramid, the chances of making a wrong investment are significantly reduced. Buying a plot where no development is there and no houses are built in nearby areas is like buying small cap stock which can give very high returns in 10-15 years but on the other side it can also very risky to buy because sometimes development will not happen in that area and returns may not be as expected. Similarly if you consider a re-sale plot where one or two houses are built in that area, you can compare this land to midcap stock which gives decent and above average return in 10-15 years. Similarly if you consider a re-sale plot where locality is already developed, you can compare this land to large-cap stock which gives average return in time duration of 10-15 years but risk is lowest in terms of price appreciation. Sometimes re-sale plots in already developed areas are highly illiquid because supply is very less so there is big difference between bids and ask price so sometimes you can get high profit from selling plots if any urgent buy required. If you are buying plot in metro city you have to make sure that the plot will be livable after 10-15 years because currently big cities are going vertical. Now builders are constructing multi-story apartment of 40-50 floors and people want to live near economic zones and they don't want to go very far from the city. If you buy plot at very far distant location from heart of metro city, it may happen that your plot will not be livable condition even after 15 years. Whenever you are buying a plot in Metro City, if possible try to buy plot of bigger size. Actually each city has some rules to construct high rise depending on plot size. For example if plot size is 125 sqyard, you can make Ground plus two floors. If plot size is 300 sqyard, you can make Ground plus five floors and if your plot size is 800 sqyard, you can make 7-10 floors. If you buy bigger plot size, number of floors increases depending on municipality rules of your city so plot appreciation will be higher for bigger size plots as builder can take more benefit by constructing more number of floors so builder can pay more to you for your plot.

CHAPTER VI

Checklist for buying property based on internet search

"Buy real estate in areas where the path exists nd buy more real estate where there is no path, but you can create your own.—David Waronker"

1. You need to physically visit property to check density of that area because if you use Google maps in terrain mode for checking density of any area you can see the covered area but you cannot get to know the actual density like number of floors or height of building. For example if in some area 4 story buildings are there but in other area 20-40 floors building are there, both layout looks same in Google maps but second type of area is may be highly density populated area.

2. For many ready to move societies you will never find property ads in online websites or only one or two ads because property demand is so much high that flats are bought by friends, relatives and residents of society by details shared in whtsapp, mygate and nobroker apps. It may also happen that property ads that you see in online portals are not easy to sell by owners or at inflated prices and sometimes owners post their property ads in property portals to check demand for their property.

3. You need to physically visit property to check whether any foul smell is coming from nearby industrial areas.

4. You need to physically visit property to check whether any nearby railway track is there to check sound pollution due to trains.

5. You need to physically visit property to check whether airport is close to check sound pollution due to flights.

6. You need to physically visit property to check whether proper ventilation and sunlight is there through balcony.

7. You need to physically visit property to check gentry of people living in that society like if you are a old couple and in that society all batchers are living you cannot easy accustomed or mingle with them and reverse also true.

8. You need to physically visit property to check whether any seepage issue in flat exists.

9. You need to physically visit property to check whether any flooding will not happen to your society or area where property situated should not be a low lying area.

10. You need to physically visit property to check which gentry or class is residing in society for example rich class or middle class. If you belong to middle class and you bought flat for end use in ultra-rich class society by getting money from inheritance then it may happen that you feel that monthly maintenance is too high for you and you have to spend lot of extra money to match status of ultra-rich class.

CHAPTER VII

Why should you buy a home even you don't like it

"The best time to buy a home is always five years ago.—Ray Brown"

Sometimes, it happens that properties you like are beyond your budget, and the properties that are in your budget don't appeal to you. In such a condition, decision paralysis sets in, and you missed opportunity to buy a property. In such cases, the advice is to go ahead and buy the property that fits your budget without over thinking. Reasoning behind this, you can understand from this example. Like you know that a low budget car may not perform as well in safety tests as compared to high cost SUV, so people might advise you not to buy low budget car as it is not safe. But if you engage in higher-order thinking, you will understand that while low budget car may not be as safe as SUV but still low budget car is much safer than riding a bike with your family. The same concept applies when you want a 3 BHK apartment but your budget is to buy a 2 BHK apartment and you don't want to buy 2 BHK as you cannot live with your parents in 2BHK. Living in own house is still better than living on rent where owner keep increasing rents each year and you have fears and anxiety that owner may evict you. While buying property, you should also consider the property's growth, price appreciation, and rental yield also. You may like a big house, but it's may happen that the rent for a big house is very low in that area or you bought a big 4BHK flat at very high price and sometimes it is difficult to sell.

CHAPTER VIII

Why prices of property in Tier-I city are high and will go higher also

"Every person who invests in well-selected real estate in a growing section of a prosperous community adopts the surest and safest method of becoming independent, for real estate is the basis of wealth.—Theodore Roosevelt"

You shouldn't choose a property based solely on your preferences. You need to pick a metro city where you are comfortable to buy and try to buy property at 15-35 minute distance from the Special Economic Zone (SEZ) as your budget allows. In big metro cities, most areas and infrastructure have already been developed, and expanding big cities is easier than developing small cities. Creating SEZs, widening of roads, making flyovers, inviting builders and big companies to small cities is challenging because they lack the systems present in big cities. Replicating the infrastructure of a big city in a small city can take 30-40 years, but expanding a big city takes only 5-6 years due to existing infrastructure, policy framework, transportation, and systems. In the future, people will prefer not to move to smaller towns since high-paying jobs, good healthcare facilities, and quality education are predominantly available in big cities. Per capita income is higher in metro cities, and people's spending is also high there. You need to choose a metro city where the per capita income is the highest. If your budget is low, you should consider buying properties in distant locations in big cities because in a few years, you won't be able to buy properties due to inflation. In the future, properties located in Metro or Tier-I cities will out price properties located in small cities by a large margin because major high-paying jobs will be in big cities and the job creation will also be higher in big cities. You can sell property in a Tier-I city and buy in a small city anytime, but selling property in a small city to buy property in a Metro city is challenging. Many people believe that just buy land anywhere in India and price will increase because land is limited but truth is that the availability of land in India is not the main factor determining the price of lands. The value of land is primarily influenced by the level of development and growth happening in a particular micro-market. As per data, India has 20% of the world's population but only 2% of the world's land so there must be great demand of land but this fact is not a direct indicator of appreciation of price of land. It requires higher-order thinking to understand that property value depend on the pace of growth and development in a specific city or area. If a city is not developing and residents of city are moving out from that city and individuals don't prefer that city for jobs and education then the price of that city can be stagnated. It may also happen that in such cases there is large difference between quoting price and actual transaction price.For example, Australia has vast amount of land and has smaller population compared to India, but property prices in major cities like Sydney, Melbourne, Adelaide, and Perth are very high. This is because people prefer to live in these major cities and don't want to go outside city limits. Outside of these cities, demand is lower and land prices may not experience significant appreciation. It's essential to consider the growth and development prospects of a city while buying property in any city. Cities with faster development, job creation, and overall growth tend to attract more people and experience higher property price appreciation. On the other hand, smaller cities or towns that have already experienced substantial growth but lack further development prospects may see slower appreciation in property values.

CHAPTER IX

How to finalize property based on your budget

"The house you looked at today and wanted to think about until tomorrow may be the same house someone looked at yesterday and will buy today.—Koki Adasi"

Your budget depends on your loan eligibility, your personal savings and any gains from selling any property or any help that you are getting from your parents. Ideally your budget for buying a ready to move flat should be 5 years of your gross salary and if it is under construction flat then your budget can be your gross salary of 6 years. For example if your package is Rs. 20 lakhs per annum then your budget will be 1Cr. If you want to stretch out it can be 6 times of your package. This formula is applicable to those who want to give 20% amount from their savings and 80% amount from Loan. Now suppose you are earning Rs.20 lakhs per annum and your wife is earning Rs.10 lakhs per annum then your total budget should be your 5 years gross salary and half of 5 year gross salary of your wife because ladies have some personal expenses and other obligations. One more thing is to consider that if your budget is Rs. 1.5 Cr then it does not mean that you should buy invest all your money to buy a flat of Rs. 1.5 Cr. If you want to buy flat at a particular location where you are sure that price will appreciate and also rentals are increasing you can go for it but if you want to diversify your risk you can buy a 2BHK of Rs. 1 Cr for your own living and a 1BHK of Rs. 40 lakhs for rental income and remaining Rs. 10 lakhs liquid cash you can have for emergency purpose or for investing in new opportunity. One other scenario will be like you invest Rs. 1 Cr in flat for self use and other Rs. 50 lakhs you can buy land with loan. Any permutations and combinations you can do depending on your savings and your loan eligibility. Sometimes it also happen that you budget is Rs. 80 lakhs but property you like is of Rs. 1 Cr. In that case you can ask money from our parents/friends for purchasing property or you can sale any existing property that is not giving good rental yields or any land that price is stagnated. It is suggested not to buy property situated at poor location. You have to consider property like Stocks you own. If any good property is not in your budget like suppose 3BHK is out of your budget then you can go for 2bhk or buy some land in any developing area so that you can buy flat after some time by selling that land. This is called hedging of properties. If you are just sitting with cash and waiting for good opportunity or confused and not able to take decision, it may possible that price of the property that you want to buy will increase more than what you actually saved in next 4-5 years. For example, if your savings is Rs. 20 lacks and your loan eligibility is around Rs. 80 lakhs initially but you like the flat of Rs. 1.25 Cr so you have short of Rs.25 lakhs. Now you try to save additional Rs. 25 lakhs in 5 years and now your total savings will be Rs.45 lakhs but it may possible that flat that cost was Rs.1.25 Cr will cost after 5 years will be Rs.1.65 Cr considering only 6% inflation per year so still you are still lagging behind Rs.20 lakhs so sometimes it is required to stay invested in real estate instead of sitting on cash. Suppose if you bought a land from your Rs. 20 lakhs saving and if it got appreciated at the rate of 15% including 8% inflation then you will get around Rs. 40 lakhs after 5 years and with additional savings of Rs. 25 lakhs and increased loan ability of Rs. 1Cr you can buy flat of Rs. 1.65 Cr.

CHAPTER X

When to visit a project for booking a property

"When you invest, you are buying a day that you don't have to work.—Aya Laraya"

Generally people used to visit any project for purchasing flat on weekends because they have offices on weekdays. It is advised to visit a flat on weekdays for booking. Reasons are as follows

1. On weekdays less number of buyers so rush is less. Brokers can easily explain about property details. Even sometimes you buy property due to rush on weekdays as you think that it should be good project as demand is very high. It might also happen that fake customers are there to give a look that demand is very high. You can never know what is happening. Salesman also gets tired on weekend to tell same information to customers. They may irritate or ignore you while answering all your questions.

2. You can analyze traffic conditions on the roads in morning or evening connecting to that property because on weekends generally traffic is less. You can check builder claims like just 15 min or 30 min drive from a centre of city.

3. Before going to buy flat, first contact to salesperson in advance on whtsapp or Email him for brochure and price list. Do a research on youtube, social media about that project or contact any advisor for getting details of that project. If you already analyze the brochure and layout details before visiting the project, you can ask your doubts to salesman otherwise salesman simply explain you about brochure and you just node your head and come back to your home. Try to visit more than one builder projects in same area so that you can do comparative analysis of multiple projects and decide accordingly.

4. Whenever you are going in search of property in any project, take your wife with you so that she can also understand the pro and cons of any project and understand your budget also and later she will not say that she don't like project. You also don't need to go again with her two times and she can also help in deciding for choosing project because it will be decision of a family. If you take your wife, brokers also think that you are genuinely

interested in property.

5. When you have decided to buy among two or three projects and you can buy one of them, go with your Chequebook and whenever you talk to salesman open the Chequebook and write name of builder. If salesman sees the chequebook with signature he thinks that you are serious buyer and he can be give you best deal or at least you can know the final rate for negotiation.

6. Try to visit in month ending or quarter ending or year ending to visit big projects because salesperson have their targets so you can get a good deal.

One more thing in last that brochures, layout plan, price list, payment plan, builder profile, information from social media and RERA Website and physical visit is sufficient for purchasing any flat. If after getting this information even you are not able to decide then you will always be confused and roaming here and there and never able to buy property and may be that property is not suitable for you.

CHAPTER XI

MIVON CONSTRUCTION

"Don't wait to buy real estate. Buy real estate and wait.—Will Rogers"

The name "MIVON" originated from a Malaysian company called "MIVON" in the 1990s. In 2010, MIVON entered the Indian market and established its presence in Mumbai. Initially, MIVON technology flats at high prices, but now MIVON technology is used to construct affordable housing flats. In MIVON technology, walls are constructed using concrete instead of brickwork. The entire structure of MIVON flats is made of concrete. Aluminum shuttering frameworks are used to create the structure, and concrete is filled inside these frameworks, resulting in a high-quality finish that's why it is also called aluminum sheer wall structure technology. In non-MIVON flats, bricks are used. Due to the capillary effect, bricks absorb moisture, and after 10-12 years, the plaster may come off the bricks. This leads to higher maintenance requirements in non-MIVON flats. After 10-15 years, the appearance of the society may deteriorate, affecting rental and resale values. After 50-55 years, residents may consider redeveloping the flats. The lifespan of non-MIVON flats is typically around 60-70 years or more, but the condition of the society and flats may not be as good as regular maintenance is required where as life of MIVON flat is around 100-120 years. There is a claim by builders that MIVON flats are hotter than normal flats because concrete retains heat. However, the fact is that MIVON flats are not hotter in reality, and this claim is not true. In non-MIVON flats, suppose if the overall cost is Rs. 100, then ratio of labor cost and material cost is Rs. 50 each. However, in MIVON flats, the costing is slightly higher at Rs. 110, but the labor cost decreases to Rs.30 because the flats are constructed quickly using MIVON technology. The construction cost is Rs. 80 due to the high cost of Aluminum frame and solid cement structure of the flats. If non-MIVON structure takes 4 years to complete then non- MIVON structure can complete in just 2 years, reducing the builder's loan cost as the flats are ready soon. So for builder MIVON(Aluminum shuttering framework) costs overall 10% extra as compared to

Non-MIVON construction but builder generally sell flats at 30-40% higher price as compared to Non-MIVON flats.

CHAPTER XII

Making informed choices in a rising Real Estate market

""Real estate is an imperishable asset, ever increasing in value. It is the most solid security that human ingenuity has devised." - Russell Sage"

If you are interested in a property in the real estate market but it doesn't fulfill all your criteria, and you are sure that the property trend is upwards in city and you understand the city's story, then you should consider buying that property even if it's not perfect. In trending real estate markets, it often happens that you may not find the ideal property within your budget, and you may have to settle for something slightly more expensive. The reason for this is that real estate prices generally do not correct significantly, and even if they do, it is usually a maximum correction of 5-10%. Reason for non-correction in real estate is due to the reason that people tend to hold their properties for a long time and don't sell them immediately. Real estate doesn't experience corrections of 30-40% like the stock market in 6-10 years. Generally, real estate goes through time corrections, where the prices stagnate, but price don't decline. In the real estate in future, property prices may be increase slowly, but the density will increase, and the size of flats will become smaller, while the rates continue to If you are interested in a property in the real estate market but it doesn't fulfill all your criteria, and you are sure that the property trend is upwards in city and you understand the city's story, then you should consider buying that property even if it's not perfect. In trending real estate markets, it often happens that you may not find the ideal property within your budget, and you may have to settle for something slightly more expensive. The reason for this is that real estate prices generally do not correct significantly, and even if they do, it is usually a maximum correction of 5-10%. Reason for non-correction in real estate is due to the reason that people tend to hold their properties for a long time and don't sell them immediately. Real estate doesn't experience corrections of 30-40% like the stock market in 6-10 years. Generally, real estate goes through time corrections, where the prices stagnate, but price don't decline. In the real estate in future, property prices may be increase slowly, but the density will increase, and the size of flats will become smaller, while the rates continue to

CHAPTER XIII

Are you a working couple and want to buy property

"The ownership of a home, the feelings of independence that comes with the possession of a bit of the earth are among the most powerful incentives to high civic interest and usefulness.— Calvin Coolidge "

Suppose you are working IT couple and you are switching IT companies in big cities like Delhi NCR, Bangalore, and Hyderabad. You did not plan to buy any property as you think that you would not stay permanently in same city. So you think that it is better to pay rent and save money and when you will be sure about living in a particular city then you will buy a flat. But in realty when the time comes, price of that property increased so much that you would think that if I had bought that property earlier it was a good decision. You regret your decision of not buying property earlier. Same happened with government employees like they think that when they will retire, they will not stay in metros and will stay in their hometown and they will never able to buy property. Whenever you delay in taking decision in buying property, property rates keep appreciating and your savings are shrinking due to inflation. If you don't know that where you will stay after 10 years you should buy small ticket size properties like small 2BHKs or 100-200 sqyd land and diversify your risk. You can also buy big land of 500 sqyd that canbe divided in 5 plots of 100 sqyard and sell it in parts because small size lands are easier to sell. You should always be invested in real estate market so that whenever you want to buy property for your own living you can sell one of your existing properties. In Stock market investing, correction can happen like Index (NIFTY) can go from 15000 to 25000 and then again come to level of 20000 so you can wait and get opportunity to invest at the time of correction and get value pick but in real estate price will not corrected 30-50% .In real estate suppose property price if go from Rs. 50 Lakhs to Rs. 1 Cr it will not correct to Rs. 70 lakhs. Property price can be stagnant for some years and this is called time correction but property price will decrease only in rare cases and moreover cost of land, construction and labor is always increasing so price of property will appreciate due to inflation. So you have to stay invested in real estate always because correction will not generally happened in real estate and you will not get opportunity to invest as price increases each year. If you are not able to decide in which city you will be living in future you can buy small plots in non-metro cities with the help and knowledge of your relatives or friends. You can also buy flat in metro city where you are living because buying a plot is sometimes a costly affair so you can buy flat and you can use it or rent it out whenever you change the city and earn passive income or you can hedge your rent.

CHAPTER XIV

Builder Buyer Agreement

"In real estate, you make 10% of your money because you're a genius and 90% because you catch a great wave." - Jeff Greene

After the implementation of the Real Estate (Regulation and Development) Act, 2016 (RERA), the builder-buyer agreement has undergone certain changes to ensure transparency and protect the interests of homebuyers. The builder-buyer agreement is a legally binding document that establishes the terms and conditions between the builder/developer and the homebuyer. Here are some key points to consider regarding the builder-buyer agreement after RERA:

1. Standardized Agreement: RERA mandates the use of a standardized agreement format to prevent unfair practices and ensure uniformity.

2. Disclosures and Transparency: The builder is now required to provide comprehensive information about the project, including project plans, layout, approvals, land title, completion schedule, and carpet area details. Any changes or alterations to the project plan must be communicated to the buyer in writing.

3. Carpet Area Definition: RERA has defined the carpet area more explicitly to avoid any confusion. Carpet arearefers to the net usable floor area within the walls of the apartment, excluding common areas like corridors, lift shafts, etc. Builders cannot charge buyers based on super built-up or any other measurement. 4. Completion Timeline: The builder-buyer agreement must specify the completion date of the project. If the builder fails to deliver the project within the stipulated time, the buyer is entitled to compensation or may have the right to withdraw from the project with a refund.

5. Structural Defect Liability: RERA holds the builder accountable for any structural defects that may arise within a specified period after possession. The agreement should clearly mention the builder's liability and the process for rectification of defects.

6. Escrow Account: Builders are required to maintain a separate escrow account for each project, where they must deposit a certain percentage of

the funds received from buyers. This provision ensures that the funds are utilized for the specific project's construction and not diverted elsewhere.

7. Termination Clause: The agreement should include provisions for termination by both the buyer and the builder. If the builder breaches any terms of the agreement, the buyer has the right to terminate the contract and seek appropriate remedies.

8. Dispute Resolution: RERA emphasizes the establishment of an appellate tribunal and a regulatory authority to address disputes between builders and buyers. It's important to note that the specification of the builder-buyer agreement can vary from state to state, as each state has its own RERA rules and regulations. Reading a builder buyer agreement (BBA) is an essential step in the process of purchasing a property from a builder.

Here are some tips to help you understand and navigate a builder buyer agreement:

1. Take your time to read the entire agreement thoroughly. Pay attention to every clause, term, and condition mentioned in the document. If there are any terms or phrases you don't understand, consult a legal professional or seek clarification from the builder.

2. Look for detailed information about the property being purchased, including the location, size, specifications, and any amenities or facilities promised by the builder.

3. Carefully review the payment terms mentioned in the agreement. Take note of the total purchase price, payment schedule, installments, due dates, and any additional charges or penalties for late payments.

4. Check the possession date mentioned in the agreement and any clauses related to possible delays in handing over the property. Understand the consequences for both parties if there is a delay and whether the builder has provided any compensation or remedies for such delays.

5. Ensure that the builder has obtained all the necessary legal approvals, clearances, and permits for the construction of the project. Look for any clauses related to refund or cancellation in case the builder fails to comply with legal requirements.

6. Understand your rights and obligations as a buyer, as well as those of the builder. Look for clauses related to changes or modifications to the property, maintenance responsibilities, and dispute resolution mechanisms.

7. Review the termination and refund clauses in case you wish to cancel the agreement or the builder fails to deliver as per the agreed terms. Understand the conditions under which you can seek a refund and any

deductions or penalties involved.

8. You need to refer builder buyer agreement to check if the club membership is open to outsiders or restricted to residents only.

9. You need to refer the carpet area, balcony area and built up area of flat in agreement.

10. If you are planning to sell flat before registry, you need to check the terms and conditions mentioned in the builder buyer agreement for selling a flat without registry and transfer charges if any by the builder.

11. You have to verify, whether car parking is open car parking or covered car parking.

12. After finalizing the deal with the builder always ask for sample copy of builder buyer agreement before giving payment to builder. Don't believe blindly on sales person regarding amenities or other facilities. You have to check these details in BBA. For example salesperson told that Clubhouse is only for residents of society but it may also possible that clubhouse facilities are also available for outside people or like clubhouse amenities are free and residents can use them just by paying maintenance per month but it can also happen that for Clubhouse facility you have to pay extra monthly. So you check these types of details in BBA.

CHAPTER XV

Buy the best and you cry only once

"Wise spending is part of wise investing. And it's never too late to start.—Rhonda Katz"

In Hindi language there is a proverb "Mehenga roye ak bar, sasta roye bar bar". It is also applicable in real estate market. Suppose you have come across a property that is priced at very lower price than the average market rate in the area. This can be seen as value for money, but you have to check thoroughly why property rate is low. Some of the factors you need to check for any property. 1. Suppose average price of any flat in any area is Rs. 7000/- per sqft. and premium builders are quoting Rs.8000/- per sqft. but you see that a property is available at Rs.5000/- then you have to investigate reasons for it. It may happen that construction quality is not up-to mark or seepage issue is there in maximum flats or RWA is fighting always or it may happen that owners of the flats of society are investor like no one wants to live in that society and all want to rent out their flats. For these type of flats re-sale is very tough. 2. For under-construction flats you need to check builder profile, reputation and quality of previous projects and completion timelines.In Hindi language there is a proverb "Mehenga roye ak bar, sasta roye bar bar". It is also applicable in real estate market. Suppose you have come across a property that is priced at very lower price than the average market rate in the area. This can be seen as value for money, but you have to check thoroughly why property rate is low. Some of the factors you need to check for any property. 1. Suppose average price of any flat in any area is Rs. 7000/- per sqft. and premium builders are quoting Rs.8000/- per sqft. but you see that a property is available at Rs.5000/- then you have to investigate reasons for it. It may happen that construction quality is not up-to mark or seepage issue is there in maximum flats or RWA is fighting always or it may happen that owners of the flats of society are investor like no one wants to live in that society and all want to rent out their flats. For these type of flats re-sale is very tough. 2. For under-construction flats you need to check builder profile, reputation and quality of previous projects and completion timelines.

CHAPTER XVI

Carpet area, Super–built up Area, Loading, Density Per Acre and Inventory Overhang

"Investing puts money to work. The only reason to save money is to invest it.—Grant Cardone"

What is Carpet area?

A carpet area is an area that can be covered by carpet inside walls. Carpet area means an apartment's net usable floor area, excluding the area covered by external walls, areas under services shafts, exclusive balcony and exclusive open terrace areas.

What is super built-up area?

The Super Built-up area of a flat is the saleable area, which includes the carpet area, along with the terrace, balconies, areas occupied by walls, and areas occupied by common/shared construction (e.g. lift, stairs, etc.). In some cases, builders include amenities like a pool, clubhouse, and garden. Builders use the loading factor on the carpet area to arrive at the super built-up area.

Super built-up area = Carpet area+area of balcony + common areas

Loading of a Flat

Super built-up area = Carpet area+ loading (area of balcony + common areas)

Loading in percentage= [1-(carpet area/super built up area)]*100 For example carpet area is 700 sqft and super built up area is 1000 then loading is 30 %. For example if super built up area is 1500 sqft and balcony area is 100sqft and carpet area is 1050 sqft then carpet area is 70% of super built up area and loading is 30%. Now for new projects you can get carpet area by adding size of rooms, kitchen and halls. Balcony area is separate. If you add carpet area and balcony area and divide by super built up area then loading will be around 30% which is ideal as per RERA.

Density per Acre of a project

Density per acre of project means total number of flats divided by total number of acre of that project. Suppose if in any project total number of flats is 400 and total area of project is 4 acre it means density per acre of that project is 100. Density per acre in a project is very important for purchasing any flat in gated society. If Density per acre is very high then too much rush will be there for using amenities like swimming pool, park or clubhouse of that society. In any occasion like Diwali , New Year, Holi if all residents come to Ground floor it may happen that no place is there for residents to enjoy that festival or due to too much rush you don't want to come to ground floor. Density per acre play also important role in time required for a Car or school bus for entering and exiting from society if we assume that each flat owner has one car. Suppose if one project has Density per acre is 110 and other is 130 then it can be comparable but if one society has Density per acre of 100 and other is 160 then this is not comparable. One more thing to consider is typography of that project like whether projects have more number of 2bhks, 3bhks or 4 bhks. If in two similar societies in one society there is more number of 3 or 4 bhks and other one has more number of 2bhk in a project then project density will be less in first one and it will be more premium society.

Inventory overhang

Inventory overhang means Number of days to be taken for inventory of flats to be sold out in current pace of sales happening in any micro market of real estate. Generally some companies like Anarock do this calculation of inventory overhang in each quarter for metro cities. If inventory overhang is less, it means either supply is less or demand is more so chances of appreciation will be higher.

Demand	Supply	Inventory overhang	Appreciation
Less	High	High	Low
Less	Less	Average	Average
High	High	Average	Average
High	Low	Low	High

Inventory Overhang effect on property appriciation

Suppose if inventory overhang is 28 months for a city, it means it will take 28 months to sale the existing inventory of flats in a city. Suppose in any micro market of any city where further inventory cannot come due to non-availability of land parcel, chances of capital appreciation are very high. For example in Mumbai, sea facing view lands are already exhausted so chances of property appreciation are very high. Fory any city, if inventory overhang is decreasing year by year then appriciation will be high and if inventory overhang is increasing year by year, appriciation will be low and reality bubble is starting to form. You can get year wise data of inventry overhang of any metro city from anarock or any other website.

CHAPTER XVII

How to choose floor or facing of flat in Multistory Apartment

""Owning a home is a keystone of wealth - both financial affluence and emotional security." - Suze Orman"

Ultimately, the choice of floor or facing in a multistory building is an individual preference. However, if someone wants to make a decision, here are some tips:

Inside facing flat Vs outside facing Flat:

Multistory flats have two types of facing. The first is inside facing, where you have a view of the park, clubhouse, or swimming pool within the complex. The second is outside facing, where you generally have a view of the road, open area, or sea. Inside facing flats provide a controlled environment; meaning what you see today is likely to be the same after 20-30 years. However, outside facing flats offer an un-controlled view. For example, if you choose a lake view facing flat, it's possible that the lake might disappear after 10-15 years if a high-rise building is constructed in between. The green lush view you see today might be replaced by new building structures in the next 10-15 years. What may seem like a green area today could turn into a construction site or a busy flyover in the future, resulting in dust and noise entering your home. Therefore, it is important to decide whether you want an outside facing uncontrolled view or an inside facing controlled view.

If you decide to go for an inside facing flat in a multistory apartment, it is recommended to choose below 10th floor i.e. the 5th, 6th, 7th, 8th, or 9th floor. The best floor among these options is the 6th floor. The logic behind this is that if you choose a flat higher than the 10th floor, you may miss out watching children playing in the park or any happening events on the ground. Also, in higher floors, the swimming pool might appear very small, and people on the ground might look tiny, which may hinder your enjoyment of the view.

If you buy a flat on the ground floor or the 1st to 3rd floor, there will be more noise from children or any activities, mosquito problems, and a higher probability of seepage issues, especially in Non-MIVON flats. Additionally, the view from the first floor or ground floor may not be as holistic. In high-rise apartments, the inside-facing flats may receive sunlight, but there could be shadows from the neighboring blocks on lower floors so this factor should also be considered.

If you choose an outside facing flat, it is better to go for a higher floor. For example, if a building has 20 floors, you can consider taking the 17th or 18th floor. Higher floors provide better views, lower noise levels, less pollution, stronger winds for good ventilation, fewer mosquito problems, and a serene environment. Some people complain about feeling dizzy on higher floors. For thosepeople, it is to mention that in new high-rise buildings, this problem is solved due to the wide balcony and the angle of the apartments. One additional solution is to place 6-inch pots (Gamla) in the balcony. By not standing too close to the railings, you can avoid feeling dizzy and stay about one foot away from the terrace. Additionally, you can use French windows, as they provide an excellent outside view.

Should I choose top floor

People often think that the top floor of a building results in higher electricity bills. However, research suggests that the electricity bill tends to be only 3-5% higher for the top floor. Nevertheless, let's assume a 10% increase. If your monthly bill is Rs. 5,000/-, that would amount to an extra Rs. 6,000/- per year. Considering this over 100 years, the extra cost would be Rs. 6 lakhs. If you are getting a discount of Rs. 5-6 lakhs on a top floor flat worth Rs. 1 Cr, then you can consider that the extra cost of electricity bills for 100 years has already been recovered in one go. Moreover, nowadays, solar panels are installed on top floors, which significantly reduce the heat on the roof. Now roof cooling paints and cooling tiles have come that reflect sun light and roof temperature can be decreased. False ceilings can also be installed, which further helps in minimizing heat. If you invest the saved amount of Rs. 6 lakhs for choosing the top floor in a multistory building and consider a 10% yearly return, it would amount to Rs. 60,000/- rupees in a year, which covers the additional electricity bill for the next 10 years.

Additionally, modern construction techniques involve multiple layers on the roof of flats, which further reduce the heating effect. The benefits of the top floor are that nobody would be partying on your roof, nobody would be flushing above your floor, and you won't hear any noise from above. If there is a lounge area on the rooftop, you may have access to it, and you will also enjoy the best view from the outside-facing top floor. Furthermore, there won't be any shadow of a tower falling on your floor because you are on the highest level. Top floors are generally considered good for Vaastu.

CHAPTER XVIII

The pitfalls of chasing perfection in property selection

" "Landlords grow rich in their sleep without working, risking, or economizing." - John Stuart Mill "

Have you remember travelling by bus in hot summer and choose a seat on the basis that sunlight in afternoon shouldn't come in through the window on your face during the journey? But after starting journey after some time, when the bus took turn, and sunlight starts coming at your face in hot summer. Now the next time when you came on the same route, you tried to choose the perfect seat again on the basis of previous experience, but this time, during the return journey, you forget that this time the direction of the Sun is reversed, and sunlight started coming in again. You carefully observed the direction of the sun for your next journey and chose a seat accordingly. However, this time no sunlight is coming at your seat but a fat guy sat next to you, causing inconvenience despite your proper planning while selecting the seat. The reason for sharing this example is to illustrate that sometime you do proper diligence and take decision but still sometimes something happen that you not expected. No property can be perfect or ideal. No matter how much you plan, minor issues may be present that you cannot predict. If you delay your decision for purchasing property by considering these minor issues, you may never be able to buy a property. Later, when the prices increase, you will regret not buying the property, thinking that if you had compromised little bit on the facing or view of the property, at least you will have purchase and holding a property.

Sometimes people give a lot of importance to amenities for example swimming pool, but in reality, only bachelor tenants, or small children use them, while senior family members rarely use them. Most swimming pools in residential complexes have a depth of about 4 feet, and they usually fill it with only 3 feet of water so no use of swimming pool actually. Similarly, even if a society has a clubhouse and gym, still people often prefer going to external gyms rather than using the one within the society, as these society gyms generally have only basic equipment or sometimes due to high density of flats in society sometimes all machines are occupied and long queue is there to use machines or equipment. Sometimes due to high density it is not possible to use clubhouse or Badminton court on weekends or sometimes these amenities are paid also separately with maintenance. Actually, sometimes people tend to focus too much on amenities and overlook the location, features and layout of flats and stretch budget too much for fancy amenities that are not sometimes useful. In reality, actual benefit of a gated society is open area, parks and security, lifestyle, social bonding which are more practical and usable for residents. Builders sometimes sell properties at exorbitant prices in the name of hi-fi amenities, but people often don't use them practically.

CHAPTER XIX

True Essence of Vaastu and solutions for Vaastu defects

"The ache for home lives in all of us, the safe place where we can go as we are and not be questioned.—Maya Angelou"

Firstly, we need to understand the depth of Vaastu and its true essence. We must understand why Vaastu was essential in ancient times. Nowadays, many people have turned Vaastu into a business of making money and spreading superstitions. The first thing to note is that the principles of Vaastu applicable in individual house does not necessarily applicable in flats. The basic essence of Vaastu is that it each house requires Sun light and ir, as positivity comes into the house through sunlight and air ventilation. There are some misunderstood facts of Vaastu and some easy solutions that can help improve the Vaastu of your flat by 95%.

SOME MYTHS OF VAASTU EXPLAINED

1. Bathroom should not be in Northeast Corner (Eshan Cone)

The first myth is that there should be no bathrooms in the northeast or northeast (Eshan Cone) corners of a flat. This rule is applicable when individual house is constructed on a plot, but it does not apply to flats. For example a 1,000 sqft flat can be a small part of project of 10-acre land so north east direction of project of 10-acre land is different and north east direction of flat is different. If we consider the direction of land of the project, the builder generally constructs roads in all boundaries of the layout and this Vaastu dosh automatically gets eliminated because in north east corner of the land, roads are there so no bathroom in north east corner of land. If you look at the northeast direction of a 10-acre land, it will be a very small part. So, it doesn't matter if your flat has its own northeast corner as a part of a larger land.

Even if a standalone four floor building constructed in a 300 sqyd plot, the small builder has to leave some space or setbacks in each direction according to the approved municipality guidelines, which eliminates this Vaastu dosh of Eshan Cone. If you are building your own house on a plot and if you leave some space in the front and back of the plot, Vasstu dosh of "bathroom in northeast" would eliminated because you have already eliminated the corners by leaving some space at front and back. If you are building a house, 90% of Vaastu dosh gets eliminated on its own if you leave some space in the front and back of the plot. In a multistory high-rise building, when you buy a flat, flat is generally situated at a height from the ground level, so flat already receives air and sunlight, which also eliminates 90% of Vaastu dosh.

Wealthy people leave space in all four directions on their plots, allowing energy and air to flow freely in all corners. By doing so, they eliminate the Vaastu problems associated with north-east corner and remove Vaastu doshas in their homes.

2. East facing Flat is best

Generally, builders charge extra for east-facing entry flats, but in reality, there is no use for an east-facing flat if there is a lift in front of entry gate or a high-rise building constructed in front of an east-facing house because you will not receive sunlight from east. Concept of east facing house is like sunlight should come to house in the morning from east direction. The benefit of an east-facing house or flat is that it receives sunlight from east direction, but if there is no sunlight coming from east direction, an east-facing flat serves no purpose. People choose flats based on the direction of the main door, but practically, it direction of door is meaningless in flats in multistory apartment. For example, if the main gate of a flat is in the east, but the balcony is in the west then you will get sunlight in the evening from west direction but you cannot get sunlight in the morning. When you buy a flat, ultimately, sunlight and air ventilation matter more than blindly choosing an east-facing flat. If you are buying a plot and building a house, you should consider the east direction because generally balcony and door are in the same direction, but if you are buying a flat, you should consider the direction of the balcony rather than the main gate. You need sunlight and air coming through the balcony. The best direction for a balcony is east, and south-east or south can also be considered. Pure west and pure north-facing balconies should be avoided because there will be no sunlight in the north, and in the west, sunlight will only be available in the evening, as the sun sets from the east towards the west by going through south east to south west. Regarding the direction of sunlight, it's worth noting that in general, the sun rises in the east and sets in the west. Sunlight is stronger in the east in the morning (6-9 AM), moves towards the west through south-east direction until noon (9 AM-12 PM), then goes towards the west from 12PM to 4 PM through south-west direction, and finally settles in the west from 4 to 6 PM. If your flat's balcony or the front of your own house faces east, south, or west, you can expect sunlight at least once a day. However, if the balcony of flat or front of the house is facing north, the chances of sunlight are very low. Therefore, the best directions for sunlight are as follows: east is the best, followed by south-east, south-west, west and north.

3. 13th Floor Superstition

The 13 number superstition is prevalent outside India and this superstition also now followed in India but according to Hindu astrology, Thirteen "Trayodashi"(In Sansktri language 13 is called "Trayodashi") is auspicious number as you heard that we use to do "PradoshVrat" for God Shiv ji on the 13th day in the lunar fortnight of the Hindu calendar.

One more aspect needs to be telling that there is no specific method to determine, which floor is 13th floor in a multistory building. For example in astrology, we count everything starting from 1, while in America, they start from 0. Like in India if it is 3 story house then we used to tell that first, second and third floor or "teen manjila makan" but foreign culture come and now we use to tell that 3 story house as ground plus two(G+2). In multistory building generally flat numbering starts from zero but suppose if numbering starts from one then 13th floor will become 14th floor so it becomes challenging to decide which floor is the 13th actually.

4. House should not be South facing

In Vastu, south-facing houses are considered inauspicious but people don't know what is rational behind this. The scientific reason behind this is that in ancient times, houses were built in the middle of large plots, and south-facing houses used to get very hot because the sun moves from the southeast to the southwest in the southern hemisphere between 10 AM and 4 PM. Hence, the sun would remain in the southern part for the maximum time. Therefore, people used to say that houses should not be south-facing. However, in modern times, plots are arranged row-wise, and all the plots are situated in the same direction, with one plot also at the back of the each house in row wise. Only the front side is open for the house and left and right side of any plot, other plots are there on which houses are built, so the problem of the house getting too hot has been solved. Moreover, nowadays, houses have air conditioning, so the issue of south-facing houses has been eliminated.

Role of Vastu and Prarabdha

Suppose there is a 40 floor building and balcony and entrance door of all flats have same direction, but one family living on 32ᵗʰ floor is suffering from health issues and that family think that the reason is bad Vaastu of their house. Then according to that notion, all the 40 floors in that direction should have bad Vaastu because all have same layout, same direction of balcony and entrance door but all families residing in all 40 floors are not suffering. Similarly, if there is a road where entrance of all the individual houses is south, then all the houses should have bad Vaastu due to south facing entry of house and all residents those are living in that houses should have suffer, but that's not how actually it works. In reality, reason for suffering is not bad Vaastu but due to "prarabdha". According to Sri Swami Sivananda:

"Prarabdha is that portion of the past karma which is responsible for the present body. That portion of the sanchita karma which influences human life in the present incarnation is called prarabdha. It is ripe for reaping. It cannot be avoided or changed. It is only exhausted by being experienced. "

In reality, the suffering of an individual can be attributed to their birth chart (janamkundli) if you believe in birth chart, which has a significant influence on theirlife. Simply correcting Vaastu alone cannot solve all the problems.

Suppose if you have a well-designed house with good Vaastu but if the house is cluttered, you won't be able to focus. If your entire house is dirty, there's no use of having good Vaastu.

It's important to understand that not every house can be perfect for everyone, so seeking a perfect house is unrealistic. In practical terms, you can make adjustments based on individual needs. For instance, if everything is going well for your mother and father but your sibling is not performing well in studies, you can change their room or bed instead of spending a large sum of money consulting a specialist. Similarly, if there is an argument in the kitchen, you can change the stove or the location where you cook food. These are small solutions to address Vaastu concerns. In life, what matters more than Vaastu is the people you live with, as they significantly impact your happiness. The quality of your mattress and bed, as well as the cleanliness of your bathroom, also play a crucial role.

CHAPTER XX

Benefits of Joint Ownership

"I advise women to invest in real estate. It is the collateral to be preferred above all others, and the safest means of investing money.—Hetty Green"

In today's time, you can manage with a small salary for food and clothing, if you already own a house but if you don't own a house, rents per months is a big expenditure and it is increasing each year and buying a "home" requires savings of your life, and many people are unable to afford it that's why you should buy house as early as possible. If you are married, it is advisable to purchase property in the names of both husband and wife because property is like insurance. In the event of death, if the property is in the names of both husband and wife, the wife will have full rights to that property; otherwise, legal issues may arise. With joint ownership of the property, at least your wife and children will have a home where they can reside, if something happen to you. If the flat or house is jointly owned and you have taken a home loan, the tax savings due to the interest on the home loan will also be doubled. Sometimes, trust issues arise among couples in the current generation, and they feel that if they buy the property in their own name, it will remain theirs in the event of a divorce. However, in the case of divorce, if the property has been purchased in one's own name after marriage, the wife also has rights in it, and the matter becomes complicated.

CHAPTER XXI

How age effect on decision of buying property

"Personal property brings you into society with men. But land is part of God's estate in the globe; and when a parcel of land is deeded to you, and you walk over it, and call it your own, it seems as if you had come into partnership with the original proprietor of the earth.—Henry Ward Beecher"

The decision regarding your property is greatly influenced by your age. For example, in your 20s, you may feel inclined to buy a property in the main city, preferably in the City center, even if it's a small house because, at this age, a home is primarily meant for relaxing or sleeping. You tend to eat out, attend parties, and your friend circle mainly consists of colleagues from the office. You don't want to travel much for going to offices, and you can share expenses for food and lodging, so you can easily afford a flat in the center of the city. You can enjoy yourself and have your workplace nearby. However, when you reach your 30s, you might feel that your needs have changed, and you require a 3BHK (three-bedroom hall kitchen) because you get married and have children and children needs space for playing. It becomes challenging to buy a big size flat in the city center, so you have desire to buy a flat or stay on rent far from the city where the rent is lower, and the flat is bigger. In 40s of your age, after working for 10-15 years, you may get irritated from your job , and you dream about a home for peace and personal space, and you desire a flat or villa which is open and greenery should be there even it is very far from the city. But sometimes, even that greenery disappears within 5-10 years when new projects are launched. After reaching in your 60s, you feel the need to live near the city because you require medical facilities, and your children are working in the main city, so you prefer to stay near them.

My advice to you is that you should try to buy a property near the city center if your budget allows, even if it's small. The rentals near the city center are excellent. Buying a property far from the city will always be feasible, but buying a property in center of the city is always challenging. You can sell the property near the city center and buy a property in the outskirts anytime, but it's always difficult to sell a property far from the city and buy one in the city center. Another benefit of buying a property in the city center is that even a slight increase in the city's radius, say by 2 km, can significantly expand the entire city's area. You can understand this through the area of a circle formula. If, for example, the city's radius is 10 km, the total area will be 314 square km. But if the city's area is increased by 2 km, the new area will be 452 square km. This means that by expanding the city's radius from 10 km to just 12 km, the area can increase by 138 sqkm. In other words, the city's area can be easily expanded, leading to oversupply. That's why it's advisable to try buying a property in the city center.

CHAPTER XXII

Ready to Move flats vs Under–Construction flats

"The only thing you are guaranteed in new construction is that it is going to take longer than they told you.—Egypt Sherrod"

The choice between ready-to-move flats and under-construction flats depends on various factors and individual preferences. Here are some key points to consider when making a decision:

Ready-to-Move Flats:

1. Ready-to-move flats are already constructed, and you can move in immediately after completing the necessary paperwork and formalities.

2. You can physically inspect the flat, its layout, amenities, and surrounding areas before making a purchase decision. There is no uncertainty regarding the final outcome or project completion.

3. Since the construction is already complete, you do not have to worry about construction delays, unexpected expenses, or changes in the original plan.

4. Ready-to-move flats are usually located in established neighborhoods with existing infrastructure, amenities, and social communities.

Under Construction Flats:

1. Under-construction flats often have a lower initial cost compared to ready-to-move flats. Additionally, there is a possibility of good appreciation in property value by the time the construction is complete.

2. When buying an under-construction flat, you may have the flexibility to choose certain design elements, finishes, or layout customization.

3. Developers generally offer payment plans for under-construction properties, allowing buyers to pay in installments or as per construction milestones.

4. There may be risks associated with project delays, changes in the layout or specifications, or even the financial stability of the developer.

5. Construction timelines can vary, and the possession date may be subject to delays due to regulatory approvals, labor issues, or other unforeseen circumstances.

6. Since the property is not yet constructed, it may be challenging to visualize the final outcome, especially if the developer does not have sample flats.

7. Construction activities in the vicinity may cause inconvenience, noise, and disruption to daily life until the project is complete.

After the introduction of RERA (Real Estate Regulatory Authority), the problem of non-construction or delayed construction of flats has been addressed. Those who have savings available for paying 20% of property price can invest in ready-to-move flats, while those who have savings available for paying 5% of property price can consider under-construction flats. This is because payments for under-construction flats are made gradually over time. Appreciation in under-construction flats are higher than Ready to move flats. Additionally, there are sometimes offers available such as 20:80 schemes, where only 20% payment is required initially and no EMI (Equated Monthly Installment) needs to be paid until possession. Ultimately, the choice between ready-to-move and under-construction flats depends on your priorities, financial situation, timeline, and risk appetite.

CHAPTER XXIII

How to use RERA Website for buying property

"Earn as much as you can, save as much as you can, invest as much as you can, give as much as you can.—John Wesley"

When a builder launches a new project, people used to hesitate to buy because they don't know the details of the project and when after sometime all details will be clear, they will not able to get good units due to delay in buying and the builder may also increase the property rates. The solution to this problem is to visit your state's RERA (Real Estate Regulatory Authority) website. There, you can enter the builder's name and project name to search for the project details. You will find the builder's application details, including information about the promoter's previous history, any criminal or police cases, past experience details, land details, built-up area details, percentage of work completed, list of mortgaged flats, name of the architect and structural engineer, copy of the legal title report, details of encumbrances, and a copy of the approved layout plan. Some of these details may not be disclosed by the salesman. If a salesman wants to hide any details from you, you can find those details on your state's RERA website. If you purchase a property in a project during its initial launch, you will get the best units. Otherwise, if you make a late purchase, the better units such as corner or higher floor units may already be sold, and you may also get the property at a higher price.

CHAPTER XXIV

Should I accept Builder's Offer of Facilities in a Flat

"The land is the only thing in the world worth working for, worth fighting for, worth dying for, because it's the only thing that lasts.— Margaret Mitchell"

If a builder is offering you facilities like wardrobes, modular kitchens, or air conditioners with flat, it is advisable not to decline this offer in an attempt to negotiate at a lower price. There are several reasons for this.

1.The rate at which the builder is providing these facilities is likely to be lower than their actual replacement cost. Builders work on a mass scale, which allows them to obtain these items at a lower cost compared to individual buyers.

2. The builder's work is professional, and replicating the same quality and finish by yourself can be challenging.

3.If the builder is offering these facilities in a under construction flat where structure is made by Mivon Technology , making any modifications later, such as drilling holes in the walls, can be difficult as the walls are made of solid concrete.

4. If the builder is providing all the woodwork, it saves you time and effort. When your flat is ready to move in after four years, if you do the woodwork at that time, it would take an additional 2-3 months, resulting in a loss of rental income. Moreover, the cost of woodwork after four years would likely increase due to inflation, possibly by at least 1.25 times.

5. Additionally, a flat that already has woodwork done will have a higher resale value and will be easier to sell if you want to sell flat at possession.

CHAPTER XXV

Should I pay high maintenance in society

"The problem with real estate is that it's local. You have to understand the local market.—Robert Kiyosaki"

Sometimes people don't want to pay maintenance. There are several reasons why living in a maintained community or paying maintenance fees can be beneficial:

1. Living in a maintained community provides a higher level of security from external threats compared to standalone properties.

2. For housewives or individuals looking for small business opportunities, a maintained community can provide an environment for opening small business setup like tiffin services.

3. Maintenance fees often cover the cost of amenities such as parks, gyms, and clubhouse facilities, allowing residents to enjoy these amenities conveniently.

4. Living in a well-maintained society can provide opportunities to interact with individuals from diverse backgrounds, enabling personal growth and the creation of valuable contacts.

5. Maintained communities generally have dedicated staff responsible for maintaining cleanliness and hygiene, ensuring a clean living environment for residents.

6. Living in a maintained community means having access to various services and facilities within close proximity, making daily life more convenient.

7. Maintained communities often offer a favorable environment for elderly parents, providing them with a sense of security and a supportive community.

8. If you need to travel or go outside for an extended period, living in a maintained community ensures the security of your flat or property in your absence.

9. Well-maintained communities are attractive to tenants, making it easier to rent out a flat. When it comes to resale, a maintained property is likely to have higher market value and demand and easy to sell property.

CHAPTER XXVI

Understanding Redevelopment and the Value of Undivided Share (UDS) in Real Estate Investments

"The land is the only thing in the world worth working for, worth fighting for, worth dying for, because it's the only thing that lasts.— Margaret Mitchell "

Redevelopment refers to the process of completely demolishing an existing building and constructing a new one in its place. When you purchase a flat, the builder gives you ownership of land as undivided share (UDS) of the land in that project. For example, if you buy a 2BHK flat with an area of 1000 sqft in a society, you will be allocated a UDS of 10-30 sqyd, depending on the number of floors in the society. The UDS tends to be lower for high number of floors due to the higher density per acre. In the event of redevelopment, suppose if the current value of land is Rs. 1 lakh per sqyd, and if you consider only 7% return per year, after 50 years, the value of land will be Rs. 30 lakhs per sqyd. Therefore, the value of your UDS, which is 10 sqyd, would be Rs. 3 crore. The builder will provide you with a slip or "Parchi" worth Rs. 3 crore. At this point, you have two options: either you can choose to receive the money or reinvest it in flats by providing additional funds based on the prevailing flat rates at that time.

Steps in redevelopment of society

Before opting for redevelopment, the society must complete a Structural Audit of the existing building. Once that is accomplished, a Special General Body Meeting is called. As per the new rules of redevelopment of society 75% of the total number of members should be in agreement with the redevelopment project before it can be officially undertaken. After that quotations from Architects/Project Management Consultants (PMC) are received and tenders are invited from developers for new construction.

A developer is expected to finish the redevelopment project as per RERA timelines with a maximum extension of one additional year. Along with the agreement, the developer is expected to give a bank guarantee of minimum

20% of the total project cost. Members residing in the building will have to move to temporary accommodation while the work is in progress. The developer usually provides alternative accommodation in the vicinity or pays monthly rents to the residents.

What are the benefits of redevelopment?

If your building is at least 50 years old or in very poor conditions, structural repair and renovation will only increase its lifespan by 4 to 5 years then redevelopment is a more feasible and sustainable choice for the long run. The market value of a redeveloped apartment is higher than that of a repaired one. Its salability and resale value increase by manifold. A redeveloped building offers wider, cleaner, newer living spaces for the residents, thus raising their standard of living.

Additionally, a redeveloped property usually gets upgraded amenities such as EV charging points, Small cubical in society for work for home, swimming pool, gym, playground, community hall, the latest security systems, firefighting systems, faster lifts and multi-level parking. If your building is in a premium area and is slated to go for redevelopment, the market value will be very high after redevelopment.

CHAPTER XXVII

Buying property for living after post-retirement

"Before you start trying to work out which direction the property market is headed, you should be aware that there are markets within markets.—Paul Clitheroe"

There is a important perspective regarding the decision to buy a villa in places like Mussoorie, Goa, or in a village to enjoy a peaceful retirement. It's essential to consider multiple factors beyond just the desire for peace and a breathtaking view.

Here are a few factors to consider when making such a decision:

1. Medical issues can arise as your age increases and access to quality healthcare becomes crucial. Consider the availability and proximity of medical facilities in the area that you choose for retirement.

2. Your children may be working in metro cities, and as you grow older, they may be responsible for taking care of you. Consider the support system available to you in terms of family, friends, and community in the chosen location.

3. Isolation can become a concern in certain remote areas or villages. Consider whether the chosen location offers opportunities for social engagement, community activities, and access to essential services.

4. Overcrowding and changes in the demographic landscape can occur over the course of several decades. Research the long-term development plans for the area to understand how it might evolve over time.

5. Think about your preferred lifestyle in retirement. Assess whether the chosen location aligns with your hobbies, interests, and desired amenities such as recreational activities, cultural events, and dining options.

CHAPTER XXVIII

Rent Vs Buy

"*If you don't own a home, buy one. If you own a home, buy another one. If you own two homes, buy a third.—John Paulson***"**

Thousands of videos and articles are available in internet for this comparison but these answers are confusing and un-satisfactory. The answer of Rent Vs Buy is simple that you have to buy. If you have one house, you have to buy another. If you have two house buy another one. After having 3 houses like one for your own and 2 houses for your children you have to ask yourself that whether to be in rent or buy house.

Like old saying is our need is ROTI KAPDA AND MAKAN In current scenario roti and kapda can be manageable there but owning a makan(house) is very tough for a middle class person. Owing a home is like Insurance to you loved ones .

If you don't have your home and you have mutual funds and stocks in your account and suppose something bad had happened to you, your family members does not know what to do with your mutual funds or stocks. If something bad happened at least they have a home to live on. First you have to buy home although it can be small home .after having home you can go for mutual fund or whatever you like.

CHAPTER XXIX

Should I consider only rental yield for purchasing property

"Real estate is the best investment for small savings. More money is made from the rise in real estate values than from all other causes combined.—William Jennings Bryan"

Generally, we consider rental yield to determine how much rent a property is generating. For example, if a property is priced at Rs.1 Cr and generates a rent of 3 lakhs per year, the rental yield would be 3%. Rental yield can be compared to dividends from stocks. Dividend-paying stocks are considered good because they distribute their existing cash flows or profits as dividends as the company knows that it may not be able to expand or grow significantly. However, some stocks take debt to pay dividends to keep them in the list of dividend paying stocks, which makes them wealth destroyers. Similarly, certain properties in good locations can provide a rental yield of 6%, which may seem very attractive at first. However, you should apply due diligence to such properties to ensure that they should not in poor condition and have a limited lifespan remaining like, 10-15 years, or check that there should be no legal issues associated with the property. This means that you should not solely rely on rental yield and consider other factors also. You also need to assess the future growth potential of the property, such as whether people will continue to desire to live in that location or property in the coming years.

For example, in the city of Kota in Rajasthan, which is known as a hub for coaching centers, the rental yield for paying guest accommodations is around 8-10%. However, with the rise of online classes, people are now opting to study from home rather than going to Kota. Therefore, if you make a decision to invest in a property solely based on the existing rental yield, it may not be the right decision because the future desire of people to study in that location is decreasing.

Which property should I buy for high rentals

Rental yields are generally higher for smaller properties compared to larger ones. For example, a 1000 sqft flat may rent for 20,000 rupees per month, while a 2000 sqft flat may only fetch 32,000 rupees per month, and a 400 sqft one-bedroom apartment may rent for 10,000 rupees per month. So smaller the property size, higher will be the rental yield.

You can take example of a shampoo pouch, where a 5 ml pouch is priced at 5 rupees while a 500 ml bottle may cost 400 rupees, but people still choose the pouch because it requires a smaller upfront payment. The same mindset applies to rental properties, where individuals prioritize their basic needs being met in smaller homes, leading to higher demand and better rental yields for such units.

You should never invest in a flat solely based on the distance from your office because it is possible that where your office is located, there may be no growth in the real estate sector or the rents may be very low. Therefore, you should consider all these factors while investing in rental properties.

One more thing to note that buying a flat does not necessarily mean you have to live in it. For example, if you have bought stocks of ITC, it doesn't mean you have to consume cigarettes. If you have invested in Nestle stocks, it doesn't mean you have to eat Maggie noodles.

Suppose your dream is to live in a 4BHK apartment in the top society of your city, which costs Rs. 3 Cr and has a rental yield of 3%, yielding an annual rent of 9 lakh rupees. Now you have Rs.60 lakh rupees for down payment but your loan eligibility is not sufficient for purchasing Rs.3 Cr flat, you can consider the following solution:

You can buy 2 flats of Rs. 1 Cr each with taking total loan of Rs.1.4Cr and total down-payment of Rs. 60 lakhs, which have a rental yield of around 4%. This will provide you total annual rent of approximately Rs. 8 lakhs. Now you require Rs. 9 lakhs rent to live on rent in your dream flat. So Rs.1 lakhs per year difference is there in rent for your dream flat and flat that you have bought. You will need to contribute additional Rs.8,000/- rupees per month only. If the rent appreciates 7% each year, the difference of Rs. 1 lakh will be zero in 1-2 years and you will be able to afford rent of your dream villa or flat in 1-2 years.

So by hedging the high rentals of your existing small properties, you can live in a larger property. Another benefit of owning small properties with high rental yields is that they are easier to sell due to their lower ticket size, and it is also easier to find tenants for such properties.

I will show you one more example.

Suppose your dream is to live in a 3BHK apartment in the top society of your city, which costs Rs. 2 Cr and has a rental yield of 3%, yielding an annual rent of 6 lakh rupees. Now you have Rs.40 lakh rupees for down payment but your loan eligibility is not sufficient for purchasing Rs.2 Cr flat, you can consider the following solution.

You can buy 2 flats of Rs. 75 lakhs each with taking total loan of Rs.1.1 Cr and total down-payment of Rs. 40 lakhs, which have a rental yield of around 4%. This will provide you total annual rent of approximately Rs. 6 lakhs. As you require Rs. 6 lakhs rent to live on rent in your dream flat so you can live in 3BHK by hedging your rents of two 2BHKs.

CHAPTER XXX

Formulas of 15x15x15 & Rule Of 72

"Landlords grow rich in their sleep without working, risking or economizing.—John Stuart Mill"

Formulas of 15x15x15

If you invest Rs.15,000 per month for 15 years with a yearly interest rate of 15%, the future value of the investment will be Rs.1 Cr.

So if you are receiving rent of Rs.15,000/- per month and you invest that rent amount in mutual fund or any index fund for 15 years , and assuming CAGR is 15% you can earn Rs. 1 Cr from rents so you can potentially benefit from both the appreciation of the property value and the additional returns from investing your rents in mutual funds.

Rule of 72

The Rule of 72 is a simple mathematical rule that provides an estimate of the time it takes for an investment to double in value, given a fixed annual interest rate. The rule states that you can know the number of years required for doubling your investment by dividing 72 by the annual interest rate.

Mathematically, the formula can be expressed as:

Years to Double = 72 / Annual Interest Rate For example, if you have an investment with an annual interest rate of 8%, you can apply the Rule of 72 to estimate how long it would take for your investment to double:

Years to Double = 72 / 8 = 9 years

According to the Rule of 72, with an 8% annual interest rate, it would take approximately 9 years for your investment to double in value.

CHAPTER XXXI

Is your house is not an asset?

"The rich buy assets. The poor only have expenses. The middle class buy liabilities they think are assets.-Robert Kiyosaki"

Robert Kiyosaki, financial educator is best known for his book "Rich Dad Poor Dad." One of the key concepts in his book is the idea that your house is not necessarily an asset.

According to Kiyosaki, an asset is something that puts money in your pocket, while a liability is something that takes money out of your pocket. He argues that most people consider their primary residence as an asset because it has value and can appreciate over time. However, Kiyosaki suggests that unless the house is generating income for you, it should be considered a liability instead of an asset.

Kiyosaki's reasoning behind this concept is that a house typically requires ongoing expenses, such as mortgage payments, property taxes, insurance, maintenance, and repairs. These expenses can take a significant portion of your income and require constant financial commitment. Therefore, he believes that unless you're generating income from your home, it's not a true asset but rather a liability that consumes your resources.

Instead of focusing on acquiring liabilities, Kiyosaki encourages individuals to invest in assets that generate passive income, such as commercial rental properties, stocks, bonds, or businesses. He emphasizes the importance of building a portfolio of income-generating assets to achieve financial independence.

A Critical analysis of Kiyosaki's Theory

1. According to Kiyosaki, an asset is something that puts money in your pocket, while a liability is something that takes money out of your pocket, which is true. According to Kiyosaki, when you buy a house by saving 20% and taking an 80% loan, money is going out from your pocket every month due to the EMI, your savings do not grow, your monthly cash flow becomes negative, and the house depreciates, resulting in no increase in its value. Therefore, according to him, you should not buy a house. However, this is

not always true and I'll explain the reasons with an example.

Suppose you are living as a tenant in a rented house worth Rs. 1 Cr, paying a monthly rent of Rs. 35,000/- with a yearly rent increase of 10%. Now, suppose you decide to buy your own house worth Rs. 1 Cr, with 20 lakhs in savings and an 80 lakh loan, resulting in a monthly EMI of around 65,000. According to Kiyosaki, if you continue to live on rent, you will save Rs. 30,000/- per month (65,000 - 35,000) and your initial savings will also be more. However, Kiyosaki did not mention that rents increase every year. If you live in your own house, the rent you pay to someone else becomes an investment in your own property. Currently, your EMI is Rs. 65,000/- and rent is Rs. 35,000/- but after 7-8 years, your rent will be equal to your EMI due to inflation. The EMI will always remain constant, but the rent will increase. If you are paying Rs. 35,000/- in rent and thinking that you are saving 40,000 by not taking a loan on a property, in the coming 7 years, you will have to bear the burden of increasing rent each year, and the rent will be Rs. 65,000/- and you will not own any property or asset. On the other hand, if you purchase a property and pay the difference between the EMI and the rent (Rs. 40,000/- in this case), gradually, year after year, this difference will become smaller and after 7 years, the rent will be equal to the EMI, and you will own a property worth Rs. 1 Cr initially and has appreciated to Rs. 2 Cr considering a 10% annual appreciation rate. Additionally, in India, when you build a house on land, the value of the land increases over time. Even if you purchase a flat, its value also increases as rents increase each year by 8-10% so the value of the flat cannot remain constant. Just like when the profits of a stock increase, the price of the stock increases, similarly, if the rent of a property is increasing, the value of the property will also have to increase in the almost same ratio. Therefore, it is incorrect to say that a house is a depreciating asset. It is possible that after 20 years, the appreciation in the value of the house or flat may not be significant due to depreciation, and the rates may get stagnated. However, at that time after 20 years, the rental yield will be around 25-30% of the capital invested considering an 8-10% increase in rental income per year, while the initial rental yield is 3.5-4%. Even in worst case if a flat is demolished after 80-100 years, the owner of the flat will be compensated based on the value of the land shared by flat owners on which the flat was built. In general, a house does not appreciate as much as the land, but the land does not provide rental income and even value of land also become stagnant after 20-25 years or just beating inflation, while a house provides rent to you or saves you from paying rent. In the case of the MIVON technology flats that are being built, their lifespan is 100-120 years and their depreciation is lower as comparison to non-mivon flats as seepage is not there in mivon construction and finishing is good.

Note: I always use the example of Rs. 1 Cr because it makes it easier for you to understand the calculations. If your budget is Rs. 50 lakhs or Rs. 2 crores, you can adjust all the numbers according to your situation.

2. According to Kiyosaki when you buy a house, you do have to pay property taxes, which is an expense that takes money out of your pocket. Robert Kiyosaki's point about property taxes is valid but if you don't pay taxes or fees you money cannot grow. Similarly, when you invest in real estate in India, you are required to pay property taxes, typically ranging from 5-7% of the property value, whether it is a residential or commercial property.

But the same expenses also occur that when you invest in mutual funds, there are charges and fees involved. Mutual fund managers generally charge an annual expense ratio, which can range from 0.4% to 0.5%. If you hold the mutual fund for a long term, such as 20 years, the cumulative expense ratio cost can amount to 8-10%. So, when you invest in assets like real estate or mutual funds, you have to bear these charges and fees. If you want to grow your money at good rate, you have to pay these charges or fee and you have no other option to skip these fees.

3. According to Kiyosaki, if you buy a house you have to pay maintenance, and repairs but suppose if you are living on rent then also you have to pay maintenance per month and sometimes you have to pay 6-12 months advance to owner also and your certain amount of money is blocked till you live on rent and owner will deduct some amount also for repairs when you leave the flat.

4. Homeownership is often associated with a sense of pride, stability, and emotional attachment. The feeling of having a place to call your own and the ability to customize and personalize your home can contribute to overall well-being of your family. These emotional and lifestyle benefits cannot measured in terms of money. Homeownership often brings emotional value and intangible benefits.

5. When you make home loan payments, a portion of the payment goes towards building equity in your home. Over time, as you continue to pay down your home loan, you are essentially saving money by increasing your ownership stake in the property. This forced savings can be a valuable long-

term asset-building strategy.

6. Homeownership also provides the opportunity to generate rental income if homeowners transfer to some other location and decide to rent out their property. This income can turn the house into an income-generating asset, potentially offsetting the expenses associated with homeownership and creating positive cash flow.

7. Owning a home can provide tax advantages that reduce the overall cost of homeownership.

8. Beyond financial considerations, a primary purpose of owning a home is to provide shelter and fulfill basic human needs like "Roti", "Kapda" and "Makan". While it may not generate income directly, the value of having a safe and comfortable place to live should not be disregarded.

9. Homeownership allows the potential transfer of wealth to future generations. Asset can be passed down to next generations, providing them with a valuable asset. This aspect of homeownership can be an important consideration for individuals looking to leave a financial legacy.

CHAPTER XXXII

Cashflow Quadrant concept

"The key to financial freedom and great wealth is a person's ability or skill to convert earned income into passive income and/or portfolio income.- Robert Kiyosaki"

Robert Kiyosaki introduced the concept of the "Cashflow Quadrant" in his book, "Rich Dad's Cashflow Quadrant." The Cashflow Quadrant is a framework that categorizes individuals into four main groups based on how they earn their income. These groups are represented by the four quadrants: Employee (E), Self-Employed (S), Business Owner (B), and Investor (I). Let's explore each quadrant:

1. **Employee (E):** This quadrant represents individuals who work for someone else and earn a fixed salary or wage. They rely on job security and promotions within the company.

2. **Self-Employed (S):** The self-employed quadrant includes individuals who work for themselves and own small businesses. Example of Self-employed individuals is Doctors, Lawyers, Charted Accountants and consultants. They have morecontrol over their income and have the potential to earn higher profits.

3. **Business Owner (B):** The business owner quadrant represents individuals who own and operate businesses that can generate income without their direct involvement. Business owners build systems and teams to run their businesses, allowing them to have more leverage and scalability in generating income.

4. **Investor (I):** The investor quadrant includes individuals who focus on investing their money to generate passive income. Investors use their financial resources to invest in assets such as stocks, bonds, real estate, or businesses, aiming for returns and cash flow that surpass their living expenses.

Kiyosaki's Cashflow Quadrant encourages individuals to strive to move from the Employee and Self-Employed quadrants, which typically involve activity giving your time to work, to the Business Owner and Investor quadrants, which can generate passive income and wealth accumulation like money will be working for you even you are sleeping. The framework aims to highlight the importance of building assets and generating passive income streams, so that as an individual your exposure will be more in the Business Owner and Investor quadrants to have the potential for financial independence.

Using the Cash flow Quadrant in Real Estate: Maximizing Wealth Generation In the context of real estate, you can apply Robert Kiyosaki's Cash flow Quadrant framework to maximize wealth. Here's how you can use the Cashflow Quadrant in relation to real estate:

1. Employee (E): If you're in the Employee quadrant, you may be earning income through your job. You don't need to leave your job initially, and your focus should be on increasing your salary because when your salary increases, your savings will grow, your loan eligibility will improve, and you will be able to buy multiple properties.

2. Self-Employed (S): As a self-employed individual, you don't need to leave your work initially, and your focus should be on developing your skills so that you can increase your consultation fees that you charge to clients. Only then will your savings increase, your loan eligibility will improve, and you will be able to buy multiple properties.

3. Business Owner (B): In the Business Owner quadrant, Kiyosaki suggests that you have to start a new business or startup. But in reality, it is a very tough task to leave a job and start your business from scratch. Leaving a job is difficult for men because there are sometimes family responsibilities or obligations. And even if you leave your job and start a business or startup, the probability of success is very low. 95% of businesses and startups fail, so if you want to enter the Business Owner quadrant, you need to buy multiple cash flow properties. The sooner you buy multiple properties and achieve positive rental cash flow equal to your salary, the sooner you can become financially free in the Business Owner quadrant. Even while continuing your job, you can become a Business Owner by having cash flow positive properties, and there is very less risk involved in this.

4. Investor (I): The Investor quadrant is focused on generating passive income through investments and increasing your net worth and portfolio. In the context of real estate, you can become an investor by allocating your capital to various real estate properties and own multiple properties and increase your net worth and you can invest your rents in mutual fund also so you will have exposure in real estate and equity both and both will be grow.

CHAPTER XXXIII

How to become a dollar millionaire or earn Rs. 7 Cr in 7 years and what is asking run rate for it

"The philosophy of the rich and the poor is this: the rich invest their money and spend what is left, while the poor spend their money and invest what is left.-Robert Kiyosaki"

To become a dollar millionaire, which means having a net worth of Rs. 1 Million dollar or Rs. 7 crore, you need to set a goal and work towards it. In India, only 0.05% of the population is dollar millionaires, which means that 1 in 2000 people is a dollar millionaire.

How to become a dollar millionaire or earn Rs. 7 Cr in 7 years

If your aim is to reach a net worth of Rs. 7 crore, then in the next 7 years, you can aim for Rs. 14 crore considering 10% annual returns, and in the subsequent 7 years, aim for 28 crore.

If you're starting from zero, you need to earn Rs. 7 crore in 7 years, which means you need to earn Rs. 1 crore per year. This translates to earning Rs. 8 lakh per month or Rs. 40,000 per day, considering 20 working days in a month. In other words, you need to earn Rs. 5,000 per hour based on an 8-hour workday. This can be compared to the run rate in a cricket match, where you need to maintain a consistent income of Rs. 5,000 per hour. By working 8 hours a day, you can achieve a net worth of Rs. 7 crore in 7 years.

The first step is to realize the value of your time, which is worth Rs. 5,000 per hour. Avoid wasting time on unproductive conversations, such as political topics, and don't allow others to waste your time either. Currently, only top doctors and lawyers earn around Rs. 5,000 per hour, but very few people can sustain such high earnings for continuous 8 hours.

If you marry a working lady then it becomes easier for you towards journey for becoming a dollar millionaire as a couple as if your wife salary is equals to your salary now you require Rs. 2500 per hour instead of Rs. 5000 per hour. One more thing to consider, if you're getting married and both families are planning to spend Rs. 30 lakhs each on the wedding, you can propose to each family to spend only Rs. 10 lakhs and use the remaining overall Rs. 40 lakhs as a down payment on a house or to invest in a property worth Rs. 1 Cr. Considering 8-10% inflation your property value will become Rs. 2 Cr in 7 years. This will bring down your target from Rs.7 Cr to Rs.5 Cr. Now if your target is owning property Rs.5 Cr, then the achievable run rate per hour would be Rs. 1,500 as working couple.

Remember, these are rough calculations and require careful financial planning, investment strategies, and consistent effort to achieve the goal of becoming a dollar millionaire.

How to become a Crorapati or networth of Rs. 1Cr in 7 years

To become a Crorepati, which means having a net worth of Rs. 1 Cr, you need to set a goal and work towards it. If your aim is to reach a net worth of Rs. 1 crore, then in the next 7 years, you can aim for Rs. 2 crore, and in the subsequent 7 years, aim for Rs. 4 crore.

If you're starting from zero, you need to earn Rs. 1 crore in 7 years, which means you need to earn Rs. 14 lakhs per year. This translates to earning Rs. 1.1 lakh per month or 4400 per day, considering 25 working days in a month. In other words, you need to earn Rs. 500 per hour based on an 8-hour workday. This can be compared to the run rate in a cricket match, where you need to maintain a consistent income of Rs. 500/- per hour. By working 8 hours a day, you can achieve a net worth of Rs. 1 crore in 7 years. The first step is to realize the value of your time, which is worth Rs. 500/- per hour. Avoid wasting time on unproductive conversations, such as political topics, and don't allow others to waste your time either. Currently, freelancer can earn easily around Rs. 500/- per hour.

If you marry a working lady then it becomes easier for you towards journey for becoming a dollar millionaire as a couple as if your wife salary is equals to your salary now you require Rs. 250 per hour instead of Rs. 500 per hour or daily target of Rs. 2000. One more thing to consider, if you're getting married and both families are planning to spend Rs. 15 lakhs each on the wedding, you can propose to each family to spend only Rs. 5 lakhs each and use the remaining overall Rs.20 lakhs as a down payment on a house or to invest in a property worth Rs.50 lakhs. Considering 8-10% inflation your property value will become Rs.1 Cr in 7 years. This will bring down your target from Rs.1 Cr to zero and you just have to earn only for paying off your EMIs in worst case but if you are not buying any property, your daily target is to save Rs. 2000 as working couple. You can achieve this target before 7 years also. It actually depends on how you earn and invest money.

Remember, these are rough calculations and require careful financial planning, investment strategies, and consistent effort to achieve the goal of becoming a Crorapati.

CHAPTER XXXIV

Flipping of properties

""The market is a device for transferring money from the impatient to the patient." - Warren Buffett"

Many people engage in property flipping and believe they can trade properties like stocks. They think that if they buy a property for Rs. 50 lakhs and sell it for Rs. 60 lakhs in 6 months, they will earn a profit of Rs. 10 lakhs through their skills. However, the truth is that these returns are driven by the booming real estate market. Flipping properties alone cannot generate wealth. In property flipping, you incur stamp duty of 6% and brokerage fees as well. If you hold the property for long duration, you can potentially receive multifold returns, similar to investing in the stock market. People used to derive a sense of excitement, satisfaction, and achievement from flipping properties, thinking they have earned a significant amount of money from their own skills. However, in reality, they only receive a small portion of the profit share, and flipping does not always work well and you can get stuck in property for very long time. Sometimes, people pay a token amount to do agreement with seller and obtain property documents and sell it at a higher price using that agreement. However, this approach also does not always yield successful results. Think of it like growing a plant, cutting its leaves before it becomes a tree, and then cutting the plant and replanting it. Just as you wouldn't switch partners shortly after getting married after conducting thorough due diligence for 6-8 months, the same principle applies to investments. Holding the property is the best option for getting multi-bagger returns.

CHAPTER XXXV

Restructuring of family assets

"Real estate is a powerful tool for building wealth because of its potential for cash flow and appreciation.-Robert Kiyosaki"

If your parents are holding such properties that have no potential for future growth or chances are there that such properties may have legal issues in the future, you need to sell them and buy properties that have growth potential and good cash flow in the future. Suppose you have a 200 square yard plot that your grandfather bought in 1995 for Rs. 2 lakh at a rate of Rs. 1000 per square yard, and now the rate of that land has increased to Rs. 1 lakh per square yard and current value of plot is Rs. 2 crore. If you are sure that there is no future growth in this plot, you can sell it and buy a 1000 square yard plot in an area that is growing at a rate of Rs. 20,000 per square yard. If you are facing difficulty in purchasing lands due to legal issues, you can buy a MIVON Construction flat worth Rs. 2 crore that will generate good rental income and appreciate in value or you can invest in some good small cap mutual funds also. This is just an example, and you need to analyze which property will give you better returns and cash flow in the future. For example, if your family owns two houses in a small city, and the value of the house in which you don't live is Rs. 1 Cr, but the monthly rent is only Rs. 12,000, giving you a rental yield of 1.5%, you can sell it and buy a property where the rental yield is 4% and the appreciation is good. These are just examples, and it doesn't mean you have to sell all your properties. You need to consider the taxation angle and make a decision after careful deliberation. If you are selling old properties, you should also buy properties and hold them for the long term to take benefit from the restructuring of assets.

Sometimes, in today's times, it also happens that people are not aware of how many properties their family actually owns. Parents often do not discuss with their adult children how many properties they actually possess and in what ratio ancestral properties will be inherited by their children after their death. If you do not discuss about properties with your children, at least you should have a discussion with your spouse about the ancestral properties and inform them about the rights they have on those properties after your demise. It also happens that relatives take possession of properties of NRIs because their parents never informed them about their ancestral properties.

There may be trust issues when it comes to restructuring assets, as parents often believe in maintaining the status quo like they don't want to sell or purchase any property and feel that if they sell their property, their children will not take proper care of them in old age so parents use to tell children that they can do buying and selling only after their death. They may also lack confidence in decision-making abilities of their children, fearing that they might make impulsive purchases or mismanage the assets, leading to financial losses. Sometimes, it becomes difficult to explain the concept of asset restructuring to parents, as they may think that you are greedy.

There are situations where you may have built a Bunglaw by purchasing a plot for 10 lakhs 40 years ago, which is now valued at 3 crores. You live on one floor and earn a rental income of 10-15k from the other floor, while your son earns 20k in a metro city at an MNC. As a senior citizen, you might feel that your expenses are already covered by the rental income, and you may not see the need for asset restructuring. However, it is important to make them understand that by selling the property for 3 crores, you can potentially earn more than 15k per month (Rs.75k per month if you consider only 3% rental yield) and also get benefit from capital appreciation.

Buying and selling decisions depend on the specific conditions and circumstances of your family. I am not suggesting that you sell your home; I am simply providing some templates or ideas to help your family grow financially. Sometimes parents say, "After we're gone, you can buy or sell whatever you want." In such cases, you need to explain to your senior citizen parents that you have many more years to live (up to 85 years). By selling assets that are not appreciating and buying assets where growth is there and cash flow are highs, your entire family can become wealthier and experience a change in lifestyle. If you feel that your parents do not have confidence in you, you can suggest them to buy property in their name or jointly with you. If the property generates rental income after asset restructuring, you can share the income, or your parents can keep the full rent. It will make them feel good as well. If you are parent reading this article and lack confidence in your children, understand that if your children want to create issues and fight, it would happen regardless of whether asset restructuring takes place or not.

It is important to explain to your parents that if they don't have trust in you, there might be conflicts and fights in the future between you and your relatives in case of ancestral joint properties. Indeed, there are instances where property documents can get lost or misplaced, and some relatives may take advantage of this situation. They may wrongfully claim ownership and sell the property, leaving you with nothing. This problem is more prevalent among NRIs. It is important to explain to your parents that your intention behind the restructuring of assets is not driven by greed but rather for the well-being and secure future of your family. Through asset restructuring, if there is an additional cash flow, you can provide better care for your parents during old age and ensure good quality medical treatment to them for any health issues. You can hire a caretaker or ensure treatment in the best hospitals, especially if you are working in metros and cannot always be physically present. As a parent, if your child is jobless or earns a low salary, asset restructuring can help generate a monthly or additional income for them. This would enable them to start their own small venture or live comfortably even their monthly salary is low.

CHAPTER XXXVI

Importance of Proper Property Document Storage and Avoiding Costly Mistakes

"The most important quality for an investor is temperament, not intellect. You need a temperament that neither derives great pleasure from being with the crowd or against the crowd.—Warren Buffett"

Never laminate property papers for keep them safe. If you laminate property papers it will not consider as original property papers. For example you cannot laminate Rupee note. If you laminate Rupee note you cannot use it. If you laminate property papers, removing lamination comes at very high cost and still you cannot recover it fully. Some people store their property papers in lockers, and over time, these papers may get damaged. If the property papers are too old and have been lost or damaged, there are a couple of ways to address the situation. One way is to obtain certified copies of the papers from the sub-registrar office. You can visit the office and provide details of the old documents, explaining that they have been lost or damaged. The sub-registrar office will then issue certified copies of the property documents, which can serve as valid proof of ownership.

Another option, if necessary, is to transfer the property to blood relations. In some states, the process of transferring property to blood relations may be free or involve minimal charges. This can be done to establish legal ownership and ensure the property is properly documented in the name of the blood relation.

If you fear that you documents can be missing at your home then don't close existing home loans and keep loan amount of 50k -70k pending and give Rs. 500 emi to bank. Bank will take custody of your documents safely.

CHAPTER XXXVII

Understanding the Margin of Safety in Real Estate

"In the business world, the rear-view mirror is always clearer than the windshield.—Warren Buffett"

If you are planning to invest in real estate and you are not sure about the future returns after 10-15 years, and there is a possibility that the investment may provide lower returns than expected, then it's important to think about the margin of safety. In simple terms, the margin of safety represents a buffer or cushion that protects investor's returns. You have to think that whether you or your child can utilize that real estate investment in the future. For example, let's assume that the flat you are considering to purchase has provided returns below expectations in the long term. In such a case, you can still use the property for your own needs. It's similar to the situation where you purchased a Swift Dzire car to use as a taxi, but the driver ran away. In a situation where public transportation is not available, you can still use the car for personal use. However, if you had purchased a commercial bus, you wouldn't be able to use it for personal purposes.

For instance, if your child is 15 years old and he will need a house after 5 years, you can consider purchasing a house. If your child resides in Metro city, they can use it. However, if he doesn't live there, you can still rent out the property to hedge and subsidize the rent expenses.

CHAPTER XXXVIII

Investing in a Property Vs Investing in REIT in Real Estate

"Never count on making a good sale. Have the purchase price be so attractive that even a mediocre sale gives good results.—Warren Buffett"

Definition of REIT and features

In theory "REIT stands for Real Estate Investment Trust. It is a type of investment vehicle that allows individuals to invest in real estate assets without directly owning or managing them. REITs pool funds from multiple investors to invest in various types of income-generating properties, such as commercial buildings, residential complexes, hotels, or industrial properties. REITs generate income through rent, lease payments, and property sales. They distribute a significant portion of their taxable income from rents (usually around 90%) as dividends to shareholders. This can provide a steady stream of income for investors. REITs are publicly traded on stock exchanges, providing investors with the ability to buy or sell their shares easily. REITs are managed by experienced professionals who handle property acquisition, leasing, maintenance, and other operational aspects. This allows individual investors to benefit from professional expertise without the need for direct involvement. REITs provide an opportunity for individual investors to participate in the real estate market with relatively small amounts of capital."

The main difference between investing in a property and investing in a Real Estate Investment Trust (REIT) is the potential risk to your capital.

When investing in a REIT, there is a possibility of losing a significant amount of your capital. A REIT is similar to a dividend-paying stock, where even if you receive dividends, the value of your investment can decrease. While you can earn monthly returns from a REIT, the overall value of your investment may decline. In India, you can check the available REIT options and check their returns 3-4 year returns and you will get to know that some

REIT are even not able to beat Fixed deposit returns and some gave negative returns also. On the other hand, when you invest in an individual property, the chances of your capital value decreasing are relatively low. While the value of the property may remain stagnant in the long term, it is less likely to decrease in value.

If you do not have enough money to purchase a large property, you can buy joint property with your family and friends and register it according to the contribution of funds in the same percentage. This process can help you gather funds for investing in a large property and allow you to benefit from collective investment. However, even in this type of collective investment, it is important to seek the advice of a lawyer so that legal and inheritance issues will not come while selling property.

CHAPTER XXXIX

Should You Consider Early Repayment of Your Home Loan?

"You will become at least as rich as the amount of good debt you take in your life.—H. J. Chammas"

Pros of Prepaying a Home Loan:

1. Paying off the loan early can result in significant interest savings over the long term.

2. Being mortgage-free brings a sense of financial security and peace of mind.

3. Once the loan is repaid, the monthly installment is eliminated, giving you more disposable income.

4. If you have existing home loan on a property on which you are receiving rent and you want to take home loan for purchasing second property with loan, then banks sometimes don't consider rents for your first property and decrease your home loan eligibility. For example your home loan eligibility is Rs. 50 lakhs and you have existing home loan of Rs. 10 lakhs and your existing EMI is Rs. 8k and rent is Rs. 10k. So, although you are getting rent more than existing EMI for existing home loan but sometimes banks don't consider your existing rents and they will decrease your loan eligibility from Rs. 50 lakhs to Rs. 40 lakhs due to existing Rs. 10 lakh loan. So it is better to repay your existing home loan before buying your second property for increasing your home loan eligibility.

Cons of Prepaying a Home Loan:

1. The funds used to prepay the loan could be invested elsewhere, potentially earning higher returns.

2. Once the money is used to pay off the loan, it becomes inaccessible for other needs or emergencies.

3. Some lenders may impose charges which can vary between 0.5% and 2% of the total loan amount for early repayment.

4. You can get tax deduction up to ?2 Lakh per annum on home loan interest repayments so if you are in 30% bracket you can save 60k per year

and if loan is joint loan in the name of husband and wife then you can save upto 120K in a year which is equivalent to yearly school fee of a child in metro city in India or it is equivalent to yearly grocery expense of a household. So you can save upto 7-8 lakhs in 6-8 years which is equivalent to registry amount of cost of 1 Cr Flat. Even you can start SIP of 10k per months if you are interested in Equity investing.

5. In the future, as India continues to grow, interest rates are expected to decrease, similar to the situation in the USA. Therefore, it is advisable not to make early prepayments of loans.

6. If you have taken loan, your documents will be safe in bank custody and prospective property buyers consider it as a safe property because having a home loan from a reputable bank can provide some assurance to prospective property buyers.

7. If you have already taken home loan, you can get additional loan on renovations or for wood work without showing any proof. You can use this amount for emergency needs like education needs or medical emergency or for paying 10% for booking amount for buying new property.

8. Good debt refers to borrowing that is considered an investment or has the potential to provide long-term financial benefits. Examples of good debt are Home loan and Education Loans. Bad debt refers to borrowing that is considered non-productive or carries a high risk of financial stra in or loss. Examples of bad debt include Credit Card Debt, Consumer Loans and Car Loans. Although, the categorization of debt as "good" or "bad" can vary based on individual circumstances, financial goals, and risk tolerance.

Ultimately, the decision to prepay a home loan should be based on a careful evaluation of your personal circumstances, financial goals, and priorities. There are lots of financial benefits of not prepaying home loan but If prepayment of home loan gives you peace of mind then you should prepay home loan because ultimately peace of mind is most important in life.

CHAPTER XL

Should You Collaborate With Others While Making Builder Floor

"Wise spending is part of wise investing. And it's never too late to start.—Rhonda Katz"

Many people often think of not buying a flat and instead purchasing their own land, constructing a building with four friends or four relatives, and dividing the floors among themselves. Initially, this may seem easy, but it is actually quite challenging because there are major trust issues involved at the beginning. Someone might take the lead in construction, and there can be significant variations in the cost of construction compared to what was initially planned. This leads others to believe that they are being charged more money. They feel that the person leading the construction initially said it could be done in, let's say, Rs. 1 Cr. , but now he is saying it will cost Rs. 15 lakhs more. The person who is working alone and putting in his hard work is blamed for the situation but in reality nobody can accurately predict the cost of construction unless he is an experienced and skilled builder. It is also possible that someone who take lead in construction use 8 mm steel rods instead of the 10mm rods in concrete structure, and others may not even notice and cheating can happen. That's why it is advisable to proceed with building a builder floor only if you have trustworthy siblings or parents involved then only youshould construct on your own, otherwise it is best to avoid. It is highly likely that it will leave a bitter taste in your mouth if you collaborate with others for making builder floors. Sometimes, it also happen that so much money is spent in construction that if you had planned to sell the builder floor to others, you won't have much left to gain from the sale. It can also happen that if you are giving contract to some builder for making builder floors, he can cheat you for compromising quality. So sometimes it is better to sell land parcel and go for purchasing flats from top builder.

CHAPTER XLI

Builder Floor Vs Multistory Calculation and Risk Reward Ratio

"In real estate, you make 10% of your money because you're a genius and 90% because you catch a great wave.—Jeff Greene"

In some metro cities , in some locations prices of plots have seen a significant increase from Rs.10,000/- per sqyd in 2015 to Rs.70,000/- per sqyd in 2022 like 7 times in 7 years. However, this does not mean that the plot prices will reach again 7 times in 7-8 years. Let me explain the reasons behind this. In this article, I am providing you calculation for a sample project in Gurugram. You can also calculate price of builder floor by contacting any builder of your area and following municipality guidelines.

Suppose you purchased a 250 sqyd plot at a rate of Rs.1 lakh per sqyd. Considering a construction area of 2.64, you will have a total of 9000 per sqft. Assuming a construction cost, which is generally around 2000 per sqft in 2023, the cost of construction will be 1.8 Cr. Adding the cost of the plot and the interest paid on a loan taken at 7%, the total cost of the property (slit plus four floor) will be Rs.4.5 Cr(Rs2.5Cr is the land value+Rs.1.8Cr is construction cost+ Rs.20L Interest from Bank).Suppose your plan is to construct builder floors in a standalone building and sell total four flats of 3BHK layout. Assuming 30% profit margins, if you construct four flats for a total of 4.5 Cr, the cost per flat will be Rs.1.1 Cr and selling price of per flat will be Rs.1.4 Cr assuming profit of 30%. As you have a 250 sqyard plot, you can construct up to 0.66 of it on each floor, resulting in a built-up area of 160 sqyard(250*.66) per floor. Deducting 20% for walls, you will have a carpet area of 130 sqyard per floor. Considering the inclusion of the staircase and lift, you will have to deduct an additional 20 sqyard per floor, resulting in a net area of 110 sqyard per floor. This translates to a 1000 sqft flat carpet area without a balcony. However, you will have a front balcony of around 150 sqft and a rear balcony of 100 sqft. Therefore, you will have a 3BHK of total carpet area with balcony of 1250 sqft , which is equivalent to a 3 BHK of 1800sqft super built up area considering 30% loading.

To determine the cost of the flat, you can refer to the price of a top builder's 1800 sqft super built up area flat, which will give you 1250 sqft carpet area(70% carpet area, including balconies). In general price of a multistory apartment of top builder has 30% higher than price of flat in builder floor apartment.

Now, you need to determine the cost of a multistory apartment in your area that offers amenities like a clubhouse and swimming pool. If the cost of constructing your standalone building is equivalent to the cost of a multistory building in your area, no one would buy your flats because they can get a multistory apartment for the same price. Generally, the cost of a multistory flat is 30% higher than that of a standalone building, and the cost of a low-rise, Semi-gated community flat with four floors is 20% higher than that of a standalone building.

You need to ensure that the selling price of constructing a builder floor on the land you are purchasing should be 25-30% lower than the cost of a flat in multistory apartment for potential buyers to be interested in your apartments. If the value of the flats you build on the land is equal to that of a multistory flat, it means your land is overpriced. In this case, you will need to hold on the land for 10-12 years before constructing builder floors to make a profit, as no other builder would buy the land unless there is a profit in building builder floors. Those who purchased land 10-12 years ago and have seen their land appreciate by 5-10 times can still make profit, as builders are buying their land for constructing builder floors. If you are buying land for self-use, there is no problem, and you can purchase it at a higher cost according to your preference. However, if your intention is to construct builder floors and sell them to a builder, you need to first check the specific size of land as per the municipality guidelines to determine how many floors can be built on it and the width of the road in front of the land. Then, you need to consider your investment horizon. If your investment horizon is long, you can expect average or good returns, but if it is short, you may incur losses. If the rate of a plot has increased from 10,000 to 50,000 per square yard, the maximum growth has likely already occurred, and it may take a long time for the land to reach 1 lakh per square yard. Additionally, the returns may be only slightly higher than fixed deposit returns.

CHAPTER XLII

Should you buy Villa or construct own house in a plot for end use

"You are not buying a home.you are buying a lifestyle.—Sarah F. Findel"

In metros, many builders are selling dreams of owning your own house in a plot and selling plots. Selling plots by builder is very easy task for them as it involves fewer headaches. They only need to obtain approval from the authorities, build roads, and make promises about amenities. However, in most plotting ventures, builders do not provide any amenities after selling all the plots and these townships become ghost towns where no one actually lives. Plot prices may continuously rise, but end-users rarely come to live in these areas, and if they live, there is a mismatch of gentry or classes of people. For example someone bought the same plot for 3,000 per square yard, while others bought it for 20,000 per square yard, due to this residents find difficulty in adjusting among themselves and society of same mindset people cannot be formed. Security and maintenance issues are also there in maximum plotting ventures as there is no monthly maintenance so society is not able to develop even after 10-15 years. Sometimes, the "greater fool theory" applies to plots, where people assume that someone will eventually buy their plot. In metro cities in outer areas of city, it will take 10-15 years for residents to start construction and so if you start construction in initial phase and living in house, there is always some construction activity taking place in other plots, resulting in sound and air pollution. That's why people prefer villa projects or societies where a cohesive society is developed, like-minded people reside, and builders provide amenities and security. Selling a plot can also be challenging as most of the sellers want money in form of hard cash. Nowadays, not everyone has black money, so sometimes it is tough to sell plots. Suppose, if you spend overall Rs. 2 Cr on building a house in a 250 sqyard plot in a plotting venture, still you won't have access to amenities such as a clubhouse, security, or parks. Therefore, there is no use in building a house in very high inflated priced plot and the risk-reward ratio is very low. If you are certain that you want to buy a house for self-use, it is better to buy a villa rather than a plot due to the availability of amenities and security and likeminded people. The price of villa offered by builder in general 50-70% higher than the total cost incurred by a individual for buying a land and constructing house of same size in same area. This is the reason why people eager to buy plots because making house in a plot is 50-60% cheaper than owning a villa, but you also have to consider that if you buy a plot and construct a house, you will not get such a community of rich families and likeminded people and that is the unique selling point (USP) of Villa. In current times due to very high demand of Villas, sometimes builder selling villa at 100% premium as compared to making own house in plotting venture, so you have to decide according to your budget. You can consider owning a plot for constructing your own villa by purchasing plot from top builder who has already executed good projects. If you buy plots at high rates, the risk-reward ratio tends to be lower because the potential for significant appreciation in value may be limited. On the other hand, if you purchase plots at growth areas in metro cities, you have the potential to maximize your profit over a 10-15 years horizon, the risk-reward ratio is higher and you can sell it at good appreciation but keep remember also that don't buy plots too far from city because now city is growing vertically due to high rise buildings. So sometimes buying plots too far from the city will not be beneficial if no growth happen in that area.

CHAPTER XLIII

Should you buy commercial properties if you belong to middle class ?

"Find out where the people are going and buy the land before they get there.—William Penn Adair"

1. Low Risk reward Ratio: You can compare commercial space in real estate to futures and options in the stock market. Just like how only 5 out of 100 people make a profit in futures and options, similarly, only 1-2 properties out of 20 are successful in commercial space because it is very risky and tricky space. The landscape of commercial space is changing very fast, so it is generally advisable to a common man who doesn't have experience or knowledge of commercial space to avoid this space if he does not have a higher risk appetite. In general, it is used to be told that commercial properties yield returns of 8-9%, while residential properties yield only 3%. That's why people are attracted to commercial properties. However, you can also earn 4-6% rental yields in residential properties if you buy low-ticket size properties, and in 6-7 years, the rental yields can increase to 8-9% with very less risk.

2. **Low probability of success:** In general, out of 5 commercial projects, one will be a super hit, two will be flops, and two will be below average. People consider the super hit as a benchmark and purchase properties based on that and after buying they will suffer. Actually selling incentives are very high in the commercial sector and the profit margins are also high. Because of the high margins, everyone gets an incentive for selling commercial property due to which many stories are published in social and print media about commercial space.

3. **Don't be a victim of assured rentals promise:** Some builders promise assured returns or rentals of 9-12% till possession in under-construction commercial properties. People get attracted by the promise of lucrative assured 9% returns like some builders offer 9% rentals for the first 5 years till possession but sometimes it may also happen that builder sell the property for at very high inflated price and adjust his loss of giving assured

returns by taking more money from you. For example if a commercial property cost is Rs. 1 Cr then builder sell it at Rs. 1.7 Cr and give 9% assured return till possession by spending extra Rs. 15-20 lakhs. However, after possession, you may not find any tenants at all and the commercial property will become a "White elephant" for you.

4. Greed for getting easy money: Generally, loans are not available for commercial properties, so only those people who got money from inheritance or got money by selling any existing property would buy commercial properties. In 85% of cases, people do not buy commercial properties with their earned money.

5. Rapid changing landscape due to online shopping: Commercial properties can be ready to move or under construction. It is advised to a middle class person not to buy either because for ready-to-move commercial properties, the landscape is changing too fast or for under-construction properties, you will not know important details like the carpet area and maintenance, which makes it too complex. In metro cities, around 10-15 years before, couples used to meet in malls, but now with the culture of living together and easy access to each other's homes or going together on trips, couples don't need to meet in malls anymore. Online shopping apps have also become popular, and people prefer online shopping for better offers and convenience, avoiding traffic and petrol expenses. Prices of items in malls are generally higher because they have to cover high rent and staff salaries. The percentage of working women in metro cities is increasing. With big players entering the commercial space, small players will not be profitable as before. Society shops in multistory apartments also used to be a safe bet initially, but now there are too many shops in that space as well. The reason is that while the number of society flats remains constant, multiple shops are available selling the same product, and the crowd within the society is limited. Generally, there used to be one society shop for 80-100 flats, but now builders offer multiple shops that cover 50-60 flats. If you buy a flat and assume a rent of 15k per month, but the demand for flats is low, you can reduce the rent and give your flat on rent or even on worst case at least you can live there but if you buy a shop and the market in that area doesn't develop or the shop owner feels that opening a shop there won't be profitable, your shop will not get any tenants on rent. Some people keep a dummy tenant in their shop to make it look like it's already rented. Following instruction of shop owner dummy tenant will tell that he is paying a good amount of rent, and you may buy the shop based on that.

However, after buying the shop, the tenant will leave. If you want to buy a shop anywhere, you need to inquire about the rent from neighboring shops and the market; otherwise, you may incur losses.

6. No Government and RWA support: If something goes wrong with a commercial property, no one will come to help you but if a big residential project is not completed at least a resident buyers community is there for support and government also take some measures for solution and media also provide assistance.

CHAPTER XLIV

Return on investment Vs Networth and Buy and hold forever Concept

"Our favorite holding period is forever.-Warren Buffett"

In general, we are taught in investments to always consider the return on investment before making any investment decisions however the investment corpus also matter for generating returns on investment. Let's consider a scenario where a middle-class person has a corpus of Rs. 10 lakhs and takes a high-risk approach, earning a 30% return on investment, resulting in a profit of Rs. 3 lakhs. On the other hand, a wealthy individual has a corpus of Rs. 1 Cr and chooses a low-risk option, such as a 5% fixed deposit, earning Rs. 5 lakhs in returns. So you can observe that the rich person, without taking much risk, easily surpasses the overall profit of the middle-class person because of their larger corpus and higher net-worth (value of total assets owned minus total liability or loan taken is considered as net-worth).

The key takeaway here is that by increasing your net worth, you can maximize quantum of returns with less risk. Leveraging is a great way to increase net worth. By taking loans against properties and using leverage, one can increase their net worth.

The basic rule of increasing net worth is to hold property for at least 20 years, ideally for a lifetime, and to sell only when there is urgent need for money. Constant buying and selling will always result in smaller profits although returns on investment can be high. For example, if you purchased a property for Rs. 50 lakhs and sold it for Rs. 70 lakhs after two years so your returns on investment is 40% in two years but for earning a profit of Rs. 20 lakhs, you would have incurred registration charges and brokerage fees of around 10%, which amounts to Rs. 5 lakhs and you also buy new property and pay Rs. 5 lakhs for registration so your actual profit would be reduced to Rs. 10 lakhs. Even if you achieved a 40% return in two years, now your actual return is Rs. 10 lakhs which is equivalent to 20% in two years and 10% in one year. However, if you bought this property on loan and pay taxes also, your real return may be lower than a fixed deposit. Therefore, generating wealth in real estate requires holding properties for the long term and having patience.

A strategy of frequently buying and selling properties can be compared to repeatedly breaking down a gold ornament to create a new one. For instance, if you give a goldsmith a 10 gram gold ornament and they return 9 gram to you, if you repeat this process 4-5 times, your 10 gram gold will diminish to 6 gram. Property transactions involve high transaction charges and brokerage fees, so if you engage in frequent buying and selling, you will incur significant losses due to these costs. Additionally, you will also be liable to pay taxes. Even if the property value has increased by 1.5 times, engaging in multiple transactions can negate your major profits.

Another example is , if you bought HDFC stock at 500 and sold it at 800, then bought another stock at 900 and sold it at 1100, and then bought a third stock at 1500. But if that stock later drops to 900, you would be stuck and would have to bear the loss. In the case of stocks, you don't fully invest in a single stock, making it easier to bear losses. However, in real estate, you invest a significant amount of money in a small number of properties, and due to the larger ticket size, it becomes difficult to liquidate. If you make a mistake, selling that property can be challenging, and a large capital amount may get stuck. One more thing that if any investment journey, if you receive good returns, it doesn't always mean that you have earned those returns by your skills or by your knowledge. Actually, the market has given you those returns based on how long you have held that investment, and it is due to your patience for holding for long-term that investments become multi baggers, whether asset class is equity or real estate.

For example when the market is in a strong uptrend, both good and bad investments tend to provide good returns. For example, in the stock market, even companies with average financial results after April 2020,(post COVID), provided good returns because the market was bullish. Property buying should be considered a long-term investment, similar to purchasing a precious diamond that you hold for forever. It is advisable to buy something that you can hold for 50-80 years, so that your next to next generation can benefit from your wise decision. We often hear stories of wealthy individuals whose ancestors bought properties that have been passed down through generations. Their ancestors did not acquire these assets easily; it required significant effort and intelligence on their part.

CHAPTER XLV

How to become High Net Worth individual using Leverage and owning multiple Properties

"In real estate, you make 10% of your money because you're a genius and 90% because you catch a great wave.—Jeff Greene"

Generally, middle-class individuals usually strive to acquire one or two properties in their lifetime, and they feel satisfied once they have their own home and a car. They keep the remaining money in the bank and do not make an effort to generate additional income to purchase multiple assets. However, if a middle-class person desires, they can build at least 6-7 properties in their lifetime, but it can only be achieved through positive cash flow properties. You can refer to the Robert Kiyosaki model in this context. We need to focus more on rental yield properties because when the EMI of the loan becomes equal to the rent, then one can buy another property. I will explain you in this chapter how to buy 6-7 properties in average life span of 25-30 years.

Template 1: If your age is 30 years and salary of Rs.1.5 lakhs per month and working in Metro City and want financial freedom at 45-50 years age.

Let's break down the investment journey. We are assuming that you are 30 years old with a monthly inhand salary of Rs. 1.5 lakhs and loan eligibility of Rs. 80 lakhs. If you have savings of Rs. 20 lakhs, you can start with a ready-to-move flat otherwise if you have only Rs. 5 lakhs savings, you can consider an under-construction flat, where the money is invested over 4 years, but the rental income starts after 4 years. With salary of Rs. 1.5 lakhs, I am assuming that your monthly expenditure is around Rs. 50k in metro city and your salary, rentals, property appreciation and monthly expenditure all these components are increasing at the rate of 7% per year as we are following conservative approach and for simplicity of calculation.

In Lakhs(Rs.)

Year	Salary	EMI for Flat 1	EMI for Flat 2	EMI for Flat 3,4 and 5	Rent for Flat 1	Rent for Flat 2	Rent for Flat 3	Rent for Flat 4	Rent for Flat 5	Income After EMI	Monthly Expenditure	Savings per month	Savings per Year	Value of Flat 1	Value of Flat 2	Value of Flat 3	Value of Flat 4	Value of Flat 5
1	1.50	0.68			0.32					1.14	0.50	0.64	7.68	100				
2	1.61	0.68			0.34					1.27	0.54	0.73	8.79	107				
3	1.72	0.68			0.37					1.40	0.57	0.83	9.98	114				
4	1.84	0.68			0.39					1.55	0.61	0.94	11.24	123				
5	1.97	0.68			0.42					1.71	0.66	1.05	12.60	131				
6	2.10	0.68			0.45					1.87	0.70	1.17	14.06	140				
7	2.25	0.68			0.48					2.05	0.75	1.30	15.61	150				
8	2.41	0.68			0.51					2.24	0.80	1.44	17.28	161				
9	2.58		0.68		0.55	0.32				2.77	0.86	1.91	22.90	172	100			
10	2.76		0.68		0.59	0.34				3.01	0.92	2.09	25.07	184	107			
11	2.95		0.68		0.63	0.37				3.27	0.98	2.28	27.40	197	114			
12	3.16				0.67	0.39				4.22	1.05	3.17	38.05	210	123			
13	3.38			1.00	0.72	0.42	0.47			3.99	1.13	2.86	34.35	225	131	150		
14	3.61			1.00	0.77	0.45	0.50			4.34	1.20	3.13	37.59	241	140	161		
15	3.87			1.00	0.83	0.48	0.54			4.71	1.29	3.42	41.06	258	150	172		
16	4.14				0.88	0.51	0.58			6.11	1.38	4.73	56.78	276	161	184		
17	4.43			1.00	0.94	0.55	0.62	0.47		6.01	1.48	4.53	54.39	295	172	197	150	
18	4.74			1.00	1.01	0.59	0.66	0.50		6.50	1.58	4.92	59.04	316	184	210	161	
19	5.07			1.00	1.08	0.63	0.71	0.54		7.02	1.69	5.33	64.01	338	197	225	172	
20	5.42			1.00	1.16	0.67	0.75	0.58	0.47	8.06	1.81	6.25	74.97	362	210	241	184	150
21	5.80			1.00	1.24	0.72	0.81	0.62	0.50	8.69	1.93	6.76	81.06	387	225	258	197	161
22	6.21			1.00	1.32	0.77	0.86	0.66	0.54	9.37	2.07	7.30	87.58	414	241	276	210	172

Initial Salary	Rs.1.5L
Inflation	7%
Yearly Returns	7%
Salary Increase	7%

Template 1: If your age is 30 years and salary of Rs.1.5 lakhs per month and want financial freedom at 45-50 years age.

With an Rs. 80 lakhs loan, your monthly EMI would be around Rs. 68k, and assuming an average rental yield of 3.75%, your average monthly rent would be 32k. If we consider a 7% increase in salary and rentals per year, your rent would reach Rs. 65k in 8 years, equal to your EMI. This means that after 8 years one property's rent would cover the EMI and you wouldn't have to contribute anything from your monthly income. In initial 8 years principal amount re-paid for the home loan will be Rs. 18 lakhs (Refer home loan amortization schedule of any Bank) so you have to pay remaining principal of Rs. 62lakhs at the end of 8 years as total loan is Rs. 80 lakhs. Now your total savings at the end of 8 year will be Rs. 97 lakhs so you have Rs. 35 lakhs left after prepayment of remaining principle of Rs. 62lakhs. You can use Rs. 20 lakhs out of Rs. 35lakhs amount for purchasing your second flat of Rs.1 Cr and remaining Rs. 15lakhs you can use as emergency fund or invest in Mutual fund or for college fee of your child or for purchasing car.

Now, in the 9th year from starting your initial investment, you would own Rs. 2.7 Cr worth of properties (First one is now worth Rs. 1.7 Cr due to inflation and second one purchased at Rs. 1 Cr.

Now again for Rs. 1 Cr property you took Rs. 80 lakhs loan, your monthly EMI would be around 68k but this time your salary increased and you are getting rent from two properties due to which now savings are increased and you saved around Rs. 75 lakhs in 3 years and principal re-paid will be Rs. 5 lakhs for home laon in 3 years so you can repay your remaining principle of Rs.75lakhs in just 3 years and make your property free from home loan.

Now in 12th year from your investment you are getting rents from two flats and you can save Rs. 38lakhs in one year and you can invest Rs. 30 lakhs as initial down payment (20% down payment) for buying Rs.1.5 Cr flat and remaining Rs. 8lakhs you can use as emergency fund.

Now, in the 13th year from starting your initial investment, you would own Rs.5 Cr worth of properties (1st one is now worth Rs.2.25 Cr and 2nd is now worth at Rs.1.3 Cr and third one purchased Rs.1.5Cr.)

Now this time for Rs.1.5 Cr property you took Rs. 1.2 Cr loan, your monthly EMI would be around Rs. 1 lakhs but this time your salary increased and you are getting rent from three properties due to which now savings are increased and you saved around Rs. 1.1Cr in 3 years and principal already paid Rs. 10 lakhs for home loan in 3 years so you can repay your home loan in just 3 years this time and make your property free from home loan.

Now in 16th year from your investment you are getting rents from three flats and you can save Rs. 41 lakhs in one year and you can invest Rs.30 lakhs as initial down payment (20% down payment) for buying Rs.1.5 Cr flat and remaining Rs. 11 lakhs you can use as emergency fund.

Now, in the 20th year from starting your initial investment, you would own Rs. 11.5 Cr worth of properties (1st one is now worth Rs. 3.62 Cr , 2nd is now worth Rs. 2.1 Cr and 3rd is now worth at Rs. 2.4 Cr and 4th one purchased Rs. 1.5Cr.)

Now this time for Rs.1.5 Cr property you took Rs. 1.2Cr loan, your monthly EMI would be around Rs.1 lakhs and you are getting rent from four properties due to which now savings are increased and you saved around Rs. 2Cr in 3 years so you can repay your home loan of Rs 1.2 Cr in just 3 years this time and make your property free from home loan and still you have Rs. 80 lakhs left for marriage or higher education of your children. Now at this stage you can buy property from your savings in each 3-4 years and no need for taking home loan for purchasing property. If you want do live a retirement life peacefully that option is also there as you are getting Rs.

4lakhs rent per month so its upto you that what you want to do in your life.

Template 2 : If your age is 30 years and salary of Rs. 70k per month and working in Metro City and want financial freedom at 50 years age

Let's break down the investment journey. We are assuming that you are 30 years old with a monthly salary of Rs. 70k and loan eligibility of Rs. 40 lakhs. You currently have savings of Rs. 20 lakhs, you can start with a ready-to-move flat. If you have only Rs. 10 lakhs, you can consider an under-construction flat, where the money is invested over 4 years, but the rental income starts after 4 years. With salary of Rs. 70k we are assuming that your monthly expenditure is around Rs. 40k in metro city and your salary, rentals, property appreciation and monthly expenditure is increasing at the rate of 7% per year as we are following conservative approach and for simplicity of calculation.

With an Rs. 40 lakhs loan, your monthly EMI would be around Rs. 35k, and assuming an average rental yield of 3.75%, your average monthly rent would be Rs. 20k. In initial 8 years principal amount for the home loan re-paid will be Rs. 10 lakhs (Refer home loan amortization schedule of any Bank) so you have to pay remaining principal of Rs. 30lakhs at the end of 8 years. Now your total savings at the end of 8 year will be Rs. 32lakhs so you can repay your complete loan and make your property free.

Year	Salary	EMI for Flat 1	EMI for Flat 2	EMI for Flat 3	Rent for Flat 1	Rent for Flat 2	Rent for Flat 3	Income After EMI	Monthly Expenditure	Savings per month	Savings per Year	Price of Flat 1	Price of Flat 2	Price of Flat 3
					In Thousands(Rs.)							In Lakhs(Rs.)		
1	70	35			20			55	40	15	180	60		
2	75	35			21			61	43	19	222	64		
3	80	35			23			68	46	22	267	69		
4	86	35			25			75	49	26	315	74		
5	92	35			26			83	52	31	366	79		
6	98	35			28			91	56	35	422	84		
7	105	35			30			100	60	40	480	90		
8	112	35			32			110	64	45	543	96		
9	120				34			155	69	86	1031	103		
10	129				37	32		197	74	124	1487	110		
11	138		68		39	34		143	79	65	775	118	100	
12	147		68		42	37		158	84	74	887	126	107	
13	158		68		45	39		174	90	84	1006	135	114	
14	169		68		48	42		191	96	94	1133	145	123	
15	180		68		52	45		209	103	106	1270	155	131	
16	193		68		55	48		228	110	118	1416	166	140	
17	207				59	51		317	118	199	2388	177	150	
18	221				63	55	47	386	126	260	3119	190	161	
19	237				68	59	50	413	135	278	3337	203	172	
20	253			100	72	63	54	342	145	198	2371	217	184	150
21	271			100	77	67	58	373	155	218	2621	232	197	161
22	290			100	83	72	62	406	166	241	2888	248	210	172
23	310			100	89	77	66	442	177	265	3175	266	225	184
24	332				95	83	71	580	190	390	4681	284	241	197
25	355				101	88	75	620	203	417	5009	304	258	210
26	380				109	94	81	664	217	447	5359	326	276	225
27	407				116	101	86	710	232	478	5734	348	295	241
28	435				124	108	92	760	249	511	6136	373	316	258
29	465				133	116	99	813	266	547	6565	399	338	276

Initial Salary	Rs.70K
Inflation	7%
Yearly Return	7%
Salary Increase	7%

Template 2 : If your age is 30 years and salary is Rs. 70k per month and want financial freedom at 50 years age

Now, in the 9th and 10th year from starting your initial investment, your savings and rent will be total Rs. 25 lakhs. You can invest Rs. 20 lakhs as 20% amount for buying property of Rs. 1 Cr and use remaining Rs. 5 lakhs as emergency expense.

Now in 11th Year for Rs. 1 Cr property you need to take Rs. 80 lakhs loan, your monthly EMI would be around 68k but this time your salary increased and you are getting rent from two properties worth total Rs. 2.1 Cr due to which now savings are increased and you saved around Rs. 66 lakhs in 6 years and principal re-paid Rs. 14 lakhs for home loan in 6 years so you have to pay remaining principal of Rs. 66lakhs at the end of 6 years. so you can repay your complete loan and make your property free.

Now, in the 17th,18th and 19th year from starting your initial investment, your savings from salary and rent will be total Rs. 88 lakhs. You can invest Rs.30 lakhs as 20% amount for buying property of Rs. 1.5 Cr and use remaining Rs. 58 lakhs as for your children education or marriage or buy car or any emergency expense or invest in equity or use it for to decrease loan amount for purchasing next flat.

Now, in the 20th year from starting your initial investment, you would own Rs. 5.5 Cr worth of properties (1st one is now worth Rs. 2.17 Cr and 2nd is now worth at Rs. 1.85 Cr and third one purchased Rs.1.5Cr.)

Now this time for Rs. 1.5 Cr property you took Rs. 1.2Cr loan, your monthly EMI would be around Rs. 1 lakhs but this time your salary increased and you are getting rent from three properties due to which now savings are increased and you saved around Rs. 1.1Cr in 4 years and principal re-paid Rs. 10 lakhs for home loan in 4 years so you can repay your home loan in just 4 years this time and make your property free from home loan.

Now, in the 23th year from starting your initial investment, you would own Rs. 6.75 Cr worth of properties (1st one is now worth Rs. 2.66 Cr , 2nd is now worth Rs. 2.25 Cr and 3rd is worth at Rs. 1.8 Cr)

Now at this stage you can buy property from your savings in each 3-4 years and no need for taking home loan for purchasing property. If you want do live a retirement life peacefully that option is also there as you are getting Rs. 2.7 lakhs rent per month so its upto you that what you want to do in your life. By investing the rental income from cash flow positive properties in the stock market, you can get exposure to equity also.

Template 3: If your age is 30 years and you are working in small city and salary is Rs.50k

Let's break down the investment journey.

Suppose you are 30 years old and your monthly salary is Rs. 50k and Rs. 5 lakhs savings in your account and personal loan eligibility of Rs. 15 lakhs. Now you can start investing in plots. Reason of buying plots in small town is because good developers are not -in small towns and lots of delay in project and quality of flat in general not good and moreover people don't want to live in flat. Appreciation of plots is very high in small town cities because investors or end-users don't have alternative like buying in flat and they don't prefer to invest in equity also so only option they have is to invest in plots . Generally for Investing in plots bank gives combined loan for construction of house and purchasing plot like 60% for construction and

40% for plot purchase so it is sometimes not possible to get home loan for purchasing plots so you can use personal loan for buying purchasing plots and repay your personal loan in each 5 years. So If you have only Rs. 5 lakhs, you can consider taking personal loan of Rs. 15 lakhs for 5 years of EMI of Rs. 32k around and buy plot of Rs. 20lakhs.

5th Year from starting of investment your personal loan is completed and your savings are increased for buying next plot.

	A	B	C	D	E	F	G	H	I	J	K	L
1					In thousands					In Lakhs		
2	Year	Salary	EMI for Plot	Income After EMI	Monthly Expenditure	Savings per month	Savings per Year	Price of Plot 1	Price of Plot 2	Price of Plot 3	Price of Plot 4	Price of Plot 5
3	1	50	32	18	18	0	0	25				
4	2	54	32	22	19	2	27	28				
5	3	57	32	25	21	5	56	30				
6	4	61	32	29	22	7	86	33				
7	5	66	32	34	24	10	119	37				
8	6	70		70	25	45	539	40				
9	7	75		75	27	48	576	44				
10	8	80		80	29	51	617	49				
11	9	86		86	31	55	660	54				
12	10	92		92	33	59	706	59				
13	11	98	32	66	35	31	371	65	40			
14	12	105	32	73	38	35	424	71	44			
15	13	113	32	81	41	40	481	78	48			
16	14	120	32	88	43	45	541	86	53			
17	15	129	32	97	46	51	606	95	59			
18	16	138		138	50	88	1059	104	64			
19	17	148		148	53	94	1134	115	71			
20	18	158		158	57	101	1213	126	78			
21	19	169		169	61	108	1298	139	86	0		
22	20	181		181	65	116	1389	153	94			
23	21	193	32	161	70	92	1102	168	104	80		
24	22	207	32	175	75	100	1206	185	114	88		
25	23	222	32	190	80	110	1317	204	126	97		
26	24	237	32	205	85	120	1436	224	138	106		
27	25	254	32	222	91	130	1564	246	152	117		
20	26	271		271	90	174	2004	271	167	129		
29	27	290		290	105	186	2230	298	184	142	80	
30	28	311		311	112	199	2386	328	202	156	88	
31	29	332		332	120	213	2553	361	222	171	97	
32	30	356		356	0	0	2808	397	245	189	106	
33	31	381		381	0	0	3089	436	269	207	117	100

Initial Salary	Rs.50,000
Inflation	7%
Yearly Returns	10%
Salary Increase	7%

Template 3: If your age is 30 years and you are working in small city and salary is Rs.50k

11th years from starting from investment your savings will be around Rs. 34 lakhs and if you take loan of Rs. 15 lakhs you can buy property of Rs. 49lakhs but we consider buying plot of Rs. 40lakhs and Rs. 9 lakhs for emergency expense or buying car or for college fee for your child.

From 13th year to 21st year from starting from investment your savings will be around Rs. 85 lakhs and if you take loan of Rs. 15 lakhs you can buy property of Rs.1 Cr but we consider buying plot of Rs.80lakhs and Rs.20 lakhs for emergency expense or college fee for your child. So in 21st year you own 3 plots worth Rs. 3.5 Cr. From 21st year to 26th year from starting from investment your savings will be around Rs. 87 lakhs and you can consider buying plot of Rs.80lakhs and Rs.7 lakhs for emergency expense.

So in 27th year you own 4 plots worth Rs.7 Cr. From 27th year to 31st year from starting from investment your savings will be around Rs. 1.3Cr and you can consider buying plot of Rs. 1Cr and Rs. 30 lakhs for emergency expense or you can buy any pension plan anything else. So in 31st year you own 5 plots worth Rs.11 Cr.

""Remember that there is no sure shot formula is there for predicting returns. All are assumptions and based on historical data. One more thing that Invest in assets that bring you peace and happiness; there's no point in investing if investment does not give you peace and happiness. Remember, life is not solely about achieving financial freedom; it's also about living and enjoying the journey. Plans may not always work out exactly as expected, and that's normal. Delays and unexpected events are part of life. Sometimes you may act early, sometimes late, and there may be instances where you receive unexpected windfall money or face unexpected expenses. Be kind to yourself and adapt your investment strategy as needed. The three templates provided are general guidelines, and you can customize it to suit your preferences and circumstances. You can take help of this excel and make your own accordingly whatever suits you.""

Note:

(i)It's important to note that if you are considering high rise, then you have to purchase only MIVON flats because in these flats your flat value will appreciate more than non MIVON flats in same locality but for 4-5 story building MIVON technology not required.

(ii) If you want to get exposure in equity is you have also option to invest your all rents in Mutual fund SIPs or half of your rents in SIP and half of the rent for repayment of home loan for getting exposure to equity portfolio also.

CHAPTER XLVI

How To Sell your old house or flat

In this article, I am sharing some tips for selling your flat or house so that you can sell your flat easily.

1. If you want to sell your house, first thing is to vacate the property ,if there is a tenant living there, as tenants generally do not want prospective buyers to come and visit home repeatedly as it causes disturbances to them. The tenant might even point out flaws in the property to discourage its sale. If the tenant is working, they may not be available on weekdays, and even on weekends, they might be difficult to reach, which can deter potential buyers from visiting the flat. '

2. If your brokerage fee is 1%, it is advisable to hire two top brokers and offer a 1.5-2% brokerage fee to both. By doing this, you can exponentially increase the reach of your property. For instance, if one broker is taking 1% brokerage and offering an extra 0.5-1% brokerage to five other brokers to sell property then your reach will become from five people to twenty five people. If you give extra brokerage, your property will sell faster and you can sell your property at 5-10% higher price which will cover your 1% extra brokerage.

3. One reason to vacate the property is to thoroughly clean and revamp your property. You will need to perform deep cleaning, clean woodwork, repair taps, doors, windows, mirrors, and locks. If the toilet is in bad condition, consider replacing it. Install fresh tiles under the toilet. Change the yellowed electrical board. Despite the appearance of the society from the outside, your house should shine and impress potential buyers. These tasks may cost up to a maximum of Rs. 50,000/-. If your property is worth Rs. 1 Cr and you are investing Rs. 50,000/-, it is a reasonable expense. Understand that when a buyer visits, he will be accompanied by a lady who will thoroughly inspect the property. By investing Rs. 50,000/-, you can potentially increase the valuation of your flat by Rs. 5-10 lakhs and sell it quickly because the first impression matters. People often judge a property even before entering it, so it's essential to make a good impression. You might have heard of the phenomenon called "flipping of property," which is common in the US, where people renovate old, run-down houses and sell them at higher prices.

4. By vacating the flat, you will also be able to focus on selling the property. Otherwise, you might not be serious about selling, and potential buyers will observe how long the property has been on the market. It's important to maintain a focused mindset when it comes to selling the flat, or else it may create the perception in buyers that the flat is not able to sell.

CHAPTER XLVII

Template for decision making

" ""In any moment of decision, the best thing you can do is the right thing. The worst thing you can do is nothing." - Theodore Roosevelt"

Changing Landscape Of New Age Decision Making And Need To Have Templates

Decision-making can be challenging in today's rapidly changing landscape where people have numerous options to choose from. The lack of proper education and training in decision-making skills increase this difficulty. Decision-making plays a crucial role in various aspects of life, including investments and marriage, education. There, I am providing some framework and mental models for taking decisions for regarding investment in real estate and it will also helpful for taking decision in various aspects of life, including investments and marriage, education.

What to do if you are not able to decide about a particular thing?

If you are unable to make a decision even after conducting proper due diligence, then the answer of decision is "NO." If you have thought extensively about buying a property, changing jobs, or getting married but still can't make a decision, it means that the available information suggests a negative answer. Suppose you specifically want to buy a property, and you have all the necessary information such as the property price, rentals, legal issues, location, your budget, and the social status of that area. If, despite having all this information, you are still unable to make a decision and more queries keep arising in your mind, it signifies that the property is not suitable for you. You can't gather much more information beyond what is already available. And at the end, you will become a victim of over thinking and will never be able to make a decision. You need to make a decision based on the available information, and if you can't make a decision based on the available information, it means that investment is not meant for you. You should consider buying a different property instead.

Are You Taking Decisions Based On Trust? | Is There A Better Way

When a seller or broker insists that you trust them and buy a property, it can indicate two situations: either they consider you a fool or a novice, or there may be some flaws or shortcomings in what they are selling. If you solely rely on trust without conducting proper due diligence, it implies that you are being lazy and unwilling to take responsibility if something goes wrong. It is important to take ownership of your decisions and perform your own due diligence before making any property purchase. Trust should be built on a foundation of verified information and thorough evaluation, rather than blind faith.

How to Select One Choice Out Of Two Equally Good Opportunities?

Using a coin toss to make a decision between two equally good opportunities is a simple and random method. To implement this method, assign one choice to "heads" and the other choice to "tails." Then, flip the coin and observe which side (heads or tails) is facing up. The thought or wish that comes to your mind immediately before seeing the result will indicate your preferred choice. If, for example, you had hoped for heads, then heads would be your answer and the choice you should go with. It's important to note that this method can help in situations where you are genuinely unsure and both options seem equally appealing.

A Secret Concept Revealed To Maximize Your Wealth Creating Chances

Generally individuals are not engaging in higher-order thinking while making decisions. Higher-order thinking refers to the consideration of the effects and consequences of a decision beyond the immediate outcome. In simpler terms, it means thinking about the ripple effects of a decision.

When you make a decision, the immediate effect is the first order. However, that effect can have further consequences, which become the second order and so on. Decision-making is never isolated. It always sets off a chain reaction. Therefore, it is important to think and consider the potential effects at different levels.

To illustrate this concept, let me share an interesting example from the 19th century, around the 1820s and 1830s about the British officers who resided in their colonies. In their colonies, there were a lot of snakes and nuisances. The officers couldn't personally go and eliminate all the snakes, so they announced a scheme. They offered prize money for each snake brought to them. When they announced this scheme, locals started killing snakes and bringing them to claim the reward. Word spread through word of mouth and people started actively participating. However, as more people joined and the number of snakes decreased but people think like this scheme is a good opportunity for them to earn money. So, instead of hunting snakes, locals started breeding them to fulfill the demand. The British, being smart, realized that as long as they kept the scheme going, it would never end. So, they stopped it, but by then, the population of snakes had multiplied.

This example demonstrates how decisions can have unintended consequences and how considering higher-order effects is crucial. It applies not only to decision-making but also to learning valuable lessons for life and making informed investment choices. By being aware of the second, third, and fourth-order effects, we can save money and potentially earn from them.

In real estate, the government generally makes decisions for the growth of a city. Now, you need to use higher-order thinking to understand the ripple effect of government decisions and how the story will play out. You have to be active, conduct your own ground reality checks, be proactive, and consider all the information and consequences. For example, if the government announces a Data Centre in a certain area of the city or creating thousands of acres of warehouse space, brokers will tell you the story that there is a proposed data center, and they will advise you to buy a plot there because that area will experience significant growth. This is your first-order thinking.

However, second-order thinking involves considering how many people will be employed if the data center is established and what will be the salaries of employees those working in the warehouse or data center. In general, data centers or warehouses spanning hundreds of acres employ only 200-300 people, and their salaries tend to be low so plots of price should not increase too much as demand is low. Now, the third-order thinking is that generally, 80% of people are unaware of these details. If you are an initial buyer, you can buy at a lower price and sell at a profit by sharing the growth story with another buyer. So, if you want to become a real estate expert, you have to do higher thinking.

For example, if we consider a trend from 10 to 100, smart money always enters at 20 and rides the trend, and exits at 70. By the time the information reaches the public, a major part of the trend has already played out. Those who enter at 20 and exit at 70 earn the major chunk of money from the trend, but not everyone has access to that information. Generally, common people enter at 50-70 will be make average or good profit. Those who bought at price of 100 see that the price has already risen from 20 to 100 so they bought at the top, and it takes a long time for them to exit.

When selecting the best option out of a random sample of finite choices

People often tend to visit multiple properties when buying a house. For example, they might look at 10-15 properties within 6 months but not find any of them satisfactory. They continue looking at properties and after some time they feel that the property that they have seen earlier was actually the best. However, sometimes the rates of those properties have increased so much that they are not able to buy them anymore because they have fixed a certain old price in their minds.

In another case, let's say you start looking for a property and you liked the third one. But after making the purchase, you feel that the fourth property was even better than the third one, and you regret your decision. The same thing can happen in marriage as well. The solution to this is to determine the appropriate sample size in the beginning.

Suppose you need to select one person out of 100 candidates for an interview. You divide 100 by Euler's number (approximately 2.718), and you get 37. Now you conduct interviews for the first 37 candidates and note down their performances. However, still you are not able to make a decision at this point. So, you choose the best performer among those 37 candidates and then continue interviewing candidates from 38 to 100. If someone from 38 to100 group performs better than best performer among 1 to 37 candidates, you choose that person. Otherwise, you stick with your initial choice if you don't want to take further interview after 37 candidates. By using this procedure, you can make the best decision based on probabilities. To make it simpler, when you divide 100 by Euler's number, you get approximately 37%. So, consider 40% instead of 37%.

For example, if you decided that you will see 10 properties and choose one property out of 10, you should look at the first four properties and remember the best among them. After that, if any of the properties from the 5th to the 10th are better than your initially chosen best property, select the new one. Otherwise, stick with your initial choice. This way, you won't have regrets, as you will have made the best decision based on probability.

Survivorship bias

Survivorship bias is a cognitive bias that occurs when we focus on the successful or surviving individuals or things and overlook the unsuccessful or eliminated ones.

Let's take a closer look at how survivorship bias can manifest in different contexts:

1. When studying successful businesses or entrepreneurs, we may overlook the multitude of failed businesses that didn't make it.

2. Survivorship bias can distort investment strategies. For example, if we examine the performance of a group of stocks or mutual funds, we may only consider the ones that have outperformed the market while ignoring the ones that failed or underperformed. This can lead to unrealistic expectations and misguided investment decisions.

3. Survivorship bias can impact career decisions when we focus only on successful individuals in a particular profession or industry. For instance, if we analyze the profiles of successful entrepreneurs, we might believe that becoming an entrepreneur guarantees success, neglecting the many failed ventures.

To mitigate the effects of survivorship bias, it is crucial to consider a more comprehensive dataset that includes both successful and unsuccessful cases. By analyzing the complete picture, we can gain a more accurate understanding of the factors that contribute to success or failure.

Focusing Illusion

The focusing illusion is a cognitive bias that occurs when individuals place excessive importance on a particular aspect of an event or situation while neglecting other relevant factors. This bias can lead us to make wrong decisions based on incomplete information.

For example, imagine you are considering moving to a new city and you focus on distance of the city from your hometown. You might overestimate the distance of city from your hometown and neglect other important factors like cost of living, job opportunities, weather of city and city's social environment.

One more example is suppose you are searching for a new house to buy and your focus is only on the view from balcony or maintenance charges per month. You are too much focused on comparing maintenance charges per month between different projects that you lost focus on most important parts of property like location of project, Super Structure type like Mivon or non-mivon and Density per Acre.

In this scenario, the focusing illusion led you to prioritize a single feature while neglecting other crucial aspects that can significantly impact your overall satisfaction with the property. To make a well-informed decision in real estate, it's important to consider a range of factors such as location, amenities, price, condition, and your specific needs. By avoiding the focusing illusion, you can make a more balanced assessment and choose a property that meets your overall criteria and preferences.

Opportunity cost is a fundamental concept in economics and decision-making

Many people do not consider opportunity cost in their decision-making process. Whenever we take action in life, we give up the opportunity to do something else, and that is called opportunity cost. For example, if you eat too many starters at a buffet, you might not have enough space for the main course and dessert. This means that if you choose one thing, you cannot choose another. The same concept of opportunity cost applies to career decisions as well. For instance, if you resign from your job to prepare for UPSC exams for five years but don't get selected, you also miss out five years of work experience, which is an opportunity cost. After five years, you will be considered as a fresher in the job market. Similarly, during the COVID-19 pandemic, if you had the opportunity to purchase a flat at a lower price, but you didn't purchase because you didn't need it at the time. Now the flat's rate has increased by 1.5 times and you missed the chance to have that property. When making investment decisions, you should consider the opportunity cost of missing out other investment opportunities. For example, if you invest in a flat, you might not be able to invest in plots or mutual funds.

A solution to this problem is to diversify your capital in different asset classes like equity, land and flats and also you can diversify your real estate portfolio in multiple locations. You can target to invest in multiple small properties for investment in real estate. This provides flexibility, and if one property doesn't perform as expected, you have the option to invest the remaining capital elsewhere.

You can also learn opportunity cost by example of eating ice-cream in shop. If you choose one flavor of ice- cream and if you don't like taste, you cannot throw ice-cream in dustbin and take another ice-cream with different flavor. So in ice-cream shops, different sample flavors are there with small spoon to taste flavors. Just like trying ice cream flavors with small spoons in ice cream shop before purchasing ice cream, you can gather information and experiences before making investment decisions.

In life, before making any decision, it's essential to explore various options and gather relevant information. Sometimes you may not find a "taste of flavors in small spoon," but seeking genuine advice from others or relying on their actual experiences sometimes may help you in taking better decisions. For example, when buying a property in a new area, explore the locality, talk to brokers or residents, and gather information as much as you can to make an informed decision.

In today's time, before marriage, when the prospective bride and groom talk for 30 minutes, it serves as a small experience to understand each other's feelings. This is also a form of "taste of flavors in small spoon." In life, there are many decisions where you may not find a "taste of flavors in small spoon," and in such cases, you must carefully consider present conditions, past history, and future expectations before making a decision.

CHAPTER XLVIII

How to Verify the Property Before Purchase

""You only have to do a very few things right in your life so long as you don't do too many things wrong.""

Checklist for verification for buying re-sale property

1. Whenever you are purchasing a resale property, tell the broker or seller that you will give the token amount only after receiving the hard copies of the original property papers with all chain documents. Chain documents refer to the historical record of ownership, including the initial ownership of the land and subsequent transactions. It's important to know who owned the property at the beginning and who has purchased it over time till the current date. You should request all registry documents related to buy-sell transactions in their original format. Inform to the seller that photocopies and scanned copies will not be accepted for verification. The seller should show the original chain documents in hard copy format. Once you have all the chain documents of the original property papers, it's crucial to verify them to a lawyer specializing in real estate document verification. Lawyers usually charge a fee of 5,000 to 10,000 rupees for this service and they verify all the documents. In many cases, individuals provide an advance or token amount without checking the documents, leading to complications later on. Requesting hard copies from the seller have the advantage that you can check that whether the original property documents are missing with the seller or if the seller has taken a loan against the property and the documents are with the bank. There are instances when property papers are kept in a locker and a dispute arises between two brothers and keys of the locker are not being with the seller. Similarly, in case of joint properties under husband and wife names can be subject to a divorce case, and if the property papers are with the wife and the husband intends to sell the property, the situation may get complex.

2. You need to verify who holds the possession (kabza) of the property. For instance, if it's a plot or land, you should check if there are boundaries established all around the plot or proper demarcation is there or not. If you are purchasing a house or shop, you should determine whether it is

currently rented out or not. Some people assume that if a property is on rent, it's advantageous as they won't have to search for tenants. However, they overlook the possibility that the tenant might have taken possession of the property, leading to disputes. In such cases, where someone is already occupying the property, you should only proceed with the purchase after ensuring the property is vacant. This prevents complications arising from disputes or tenant-related issues affecting the property's sale.

3. You should verify whether there is an existing loan on the property. You can inquire directly with the seller or check the CERSAI website for confirmation. If the buyer have original property papers, it's generally a confirmation that there is no ongoing loan. If the buyer informs you that there is a loan on the property, you should request three documents from the seller: the loan statement, a list of property documents held by the bank, and a loan foreclosure letter that outlines the amount required for clearing the loan. Subsequently, you should inquire with the seller about how they will complete the outstanding principal loan. It is advisable not to proceed with the property purchase until the bank issues a No Objection Certificate (NOC) and returns the original documents to the seller. This is because there's a possibility that if the loan is ongoing and the seller has failed to pay EMIs for 7-8 months, the loan could have turned into a Non-Performing Asset (NPA), leading the bank to initiate an auction process.

4. Whenever you are purchasing any property, you can obtain an encumbrance certificate from the local sub-registrar's office. This will help you determine if there are any charges on the property.

5. Whenever you are buying property, before making the purchase, request the sellers to provide you with self-attested copies of their PAN card, Aadhar card and cancelled cheque. You can use these documents to verify the authenticity of the sellers' signatures on the sale deeds and also verify their bank account details. This step adds an extra layer of verification and security to the property transaction process.

6. When signing an agreement as a buyer, ensure that all sellers' names are included. Each seller's name and signature should be present in the sale agreement, matching the names on the property registry. Allocate the agreement amount proportionally based on the sellers' ownership ratio. For example, in a joint property owned equally by a husband and wife, distribute the amount equally. After completing the property purchase, distribute the full payment among sellers according to their ownership shares to avoid future disputes.

7. When buying a house, verify with the municipality about the ownership mutation details. Request house tax receipts from the seller to confirm whether they have paid their dues.

8. Before purchasing a property, visit the registrar office to ensure no restrictions on buying or selling on that property. Verify if the government has suspended property registration in that area or if any illegal structures or ongoing cases are associated with the property.

9. If you're purchasing a flat in a multi-story apartment, it's important to check any pending maintenance dues in RWA (Resident Welfare Association) associated with the flat. It may also happen that sometimes conflicts also arise between the RWA and the builder, leading to legal battles. Even though the property itself might not be disputed, you might need to pay regular court fees to the RWA and actively participate in any ongoing protests or disputes. One more thing to discuss with seller is car parking. Sometimes, car parking is a point of contention in multi-story apartments. Make sure to discuss with the seller whether a separate car parking space is mentioned in the sale deed. This can help you avoid any issues related to parking rights in the future.

10. When you purchase a flat, the usual process involves the builder providing you with a Builder-Buyer Agreement. Later, after the agreement, the property is registered in your name through a sale deed. During the flat purchase process, it's advisable to ask the builder for the link documents or chain of documents. These documents reveal the legal ownership history of the land on which the flat is being constructed. Understanding the land's ownership and history through these link documents is advantageous for several reasons as it enables you to verify whether the land where the flat is being built has any legal disputes or conflicts. Secondly if you decide to sell the flat in the future (e.g., after 20 years), having these link documents readily available will be beneficial for potential buyers and for taking banks loan also. By obtaining and retaining these link documents, you ensure transparency and facilitate smoother future transactions by having a clear record of the property's history.

11. If you are purchasing a property for an amount exceeding Rs. 50 lakhs, it is the responsibility of the buyer to deduct Tax Deducted at Source (TDS) as per the Income Tax Act. Failure to do so can lead to penalties imposed on the buyer.

12. If you purchase a flat in a multistory apartment and the builder does not possess an "Occupation Certificate" or "Completion Certificate," you

could find yourself deprived of several rights in case a dispute arises later. These certificates are crucial documents that signify the legal compliance and completion of the building as per the local regulations. Without them, you might face potential legal issues down the line. It's important to ensure that you should obtain these certificates before purchase while buying resale flat.

13. Whenever you are considering purchasing a property, it's a good idea to take a small loan from a bank. Banks conduct thorough property verification processes, which add an extra layer of assurance regarding the property's legality and authenticity. This step contributes to making the property transaction relatively safer and more secure.

14. Whenever you're buying property, it's advisable to meet or have a phone conversation with all the sellers involved. This step is important because you never know if any of the sellers have passed away or undergone changes in their circumstances. For instance, if a property was in the mother's name and she passed away, her son might have included his name in the agreement, accessed her bank account, and even obtained a General Power of Attorney (GPA) in her name. By directly communicating with the sellers, you can ensure that the information is accurate and up-to-date, avoiding potential complications arising from such situations.

15. When you're in the process of buying property and the rate has been finalized, if possible, try to meet with the seller before the property registration (registry) takes place. If the broker is not facilitating the meeting with the seller, let the broker know that no further rate discussions will be done by you while meeting with seller and broker commission share will remain unchanged. Meeting the seller in person allows you to verify if the person is same individual or if there is any discrepancy from photograph in sale deed.

16. If you are purchasing land and you want to check physical possession, you can communicate with the seller that after giving token amount, you wish to do land demarcation or make boundary of that land. If the boundary is already marked, you can ask seller that you will increase the height of that boundary and then proceed to complete the property registration process within 1 to 3 months. This approach helps to ensure that any potential disputes related to the property become evident after the boundaries have been clearly defined because if any dispute is there, chances that other party will come to fight or oppose the demarcation.

17. When purchasing land, after demarcating the boundaries make sure to write your name on the land. This is crucial because in many cases, the area might undergo significant development over the span of 10-15 years, making it challenging to locate your plot. By having your name marked within the boundaries, the chances of someone else fraudulently selling your plot become significantly lower. This step acts as a safeguard against potential land-related disputes in the future.

Don't Commit These Mistakes in Property Sale Agreement :

In general, a sale agreement outlines details such as the seller's and purchaser's names, the property's total price, the amount of the advance payment, and a statement indicating no existing loan on the property. It might also specify a timeframe for property purchase, typically within 45 days. However, mistakes due to oversights can happen even if you believe that all procedures have been done correctly. Here are some precautions to consider while drafting a sale agreement:

1. In the sale agreement, all sellers' and the buyer's names should be accurately mentioned, without any omissions. It's essential for all parties' names to be spelled correctly, and their signatures should be present. If there's a difference between Aadhaar and PAN details, the name from the previous registry should be used in the agreement, with the Aadhaar and PAN numbers mentioned in brackets. Signatures of both the sellers and the buyer need to be obtained on all pages of the agreement.

2. One witness should be known individual from the buyer's side, and the other witness should be known individual from the seller's side. This ensures a balanced and legally valid agreement.

3. Absolutely, it's crucial to carefully read and understand all the terms and conditions of the sale agreement. Don't simply sign it as a formality. Each clause in the agreement holds significance. If you find any terms unclear, it's advisable to consult a lawyer.

4. Generally, the default template of the agreement states that there is no charge or bank loan on the property. However, in reality, many times there might be an existing bank loan when you sign the agreement. Even if both the buyer and seller knows that property is mortgaged still they often don't remove this clause. In this regard, it is advised that if there is ongoing loan on the property, it should be clearly mentioned in the agreement that property is mortgaged. The seller should commit to completing the loan repayment, providing a no dues certificate, and delivering the original property documents by a specific date. This approach ensures clarity and

safeguards the interests of both parties.

5. If the property you are buying is currently rented, you should mention in the agreement that the property is under rent. After the sale, the rent agreement or leave and license agreement will be revised accordingly.

6. Whenever there's a sale agreement, make sure to include the legal heirs of both the seller and the buyer. The benefit of doing this is suppose if either the seller or buyer passes away after the agreement, the responsibility of payment and receipt of funds will be clear. Adding the names of legal heirs can help you avoid potential legal complications in case of any unfortunate events.

7. In a property transaction involving multiple sellers and English language is used in sale agreement, if one of the sellers is not proficient in English, there's a possibility that later on he could raise a legal concern in court, stating his inability to understand English. In such a scenario, if there's a seller who has difficulty with reading and writing English, you can consider creating an affidavit stating that this individual is your relative and he doesn't understand English, but you have explained the agreement to them in Hindi. Having such an affidavit can help safeguard you from potential legal issues.

8. Whenever you are buying property, it's advisable to avoid cash transactions as it is legally wrong and risky. Many people opt for a "kaccha agreement" (informal agreement) initially in cash transactions, followed by a "pakka agreement" (formal agreement). In such cases, the seller might refuse to proceed with the registry after receiving cash at the time of agreement or there's a possibility that if seller pass away after receiving cash payment, you could be left with just the payment slip of the "kaccha agreement". This means you won't receive the property or get back the cash that you've given to the seller.

9. If you are entering into an agreement to sell, try to get it registered if possible. While both notarized and registered agreements are valid, the authenticity of a registered agreement is higher. Registering an agreement enhances its validity, authenticity and your rights making it significantly more powerful than a notarized agreement. In cases where a seller enters into agreements with multiple parties and takes advances from them, having a registered agreement will hold more weight in court and the court will give more importance to your registeredagreement. When an agreement is registered, no party can easily deny its terms and conditions.

10. Whenever you transfer money for an agreement, the funds should be transferred from the buyer's account to the seller's account, following the same ratio as the ownership rights of the property held by the sellers and buyers.

11. Whenever you are buying property from a seller, you can include a clause in the agreement stating that if the buyer incurs any losses due to title issues or any other reasons after the purchase, the seller will be held responsible. This clause acts as indemnity or protection for the buyer against potential damages or losses. It's a promise in the agreement that the seller will cover any losses that the buyer may experience. For instance, if the agreement states that the property has no title issues, no existing bank loans, and no previous agreements with other parties, but after the purchase, title issues arise or the property is found to be mortgaged, any resulting losses for the buyer would be compensated by the seller.

12. Many times, it happens that after the agreement is finalized, either the seller or the buyer doesn't complete the property registration within the agreed time period. If the buyer fails to register, the issue is not as significant because the seller can forfeit the token amount. However, if the seller fails to register, the buyer has only option to file a suit in court under the Specific Relief Act, seeking specific performance of the contract. This means the court could enforce the seller to carry out the terms of the agreement and complete the property registration.

Precautions on the time of registration of property

Usually, on the day of property registration, people tend to get caught up in a hurried atmosphere. Given that property transactions are significant and require careful planning, it's easy to overlook certain things. Here are some aspects to keep in mind:

1. One day before the property registration, make sure to thoroughly read the draft of the sale deed and verify all details. If any typographical errors occur, later it can become major issue. Therefore, it's essential to read the sale deed carefully at least once. If you're having trouble understanding any clauses, consider getting the document verified by a lawyer.

2. On the day of the property registration, the transfer of existing property papers and old link documents takes place between the seller and buyer. In such cases, the seller can have the buyer sign on a stamp paper to acknowledge the receipt of the documents. You can create a list of documents and have the buyer sign on that list. This has the advantage that the buyer cannot later claim that the seller did not provide the documents,

and similarly, the seller cannot say that they provided the documents without any proof. This is beneficial for both the seller and the buyer.

3. Whenever you go to register the property, bring a known person with you as a witness. People often pay around 500 Rs to unknown individuals at the registration office to act as witnesses, and later, these witnesses are often unavailable in case of disputes. It's advisable to have one witness from the buyer's side and another from the seller's side. Try to avoid choosing a close relative as a witness.

4. Whenever you pay the stamp duty, cross-verify to ensure that the stamp duty is not less than the required amount. You can pay an excess amount for stamp duty, but the paid amount should never be less than the required stamp duty.

5. Whenever you're making payment for property registration, try to make the payment through RTGS or bank draft. Sometimes, cheque payments can face issues like signature mismatch or bouncing, which can lead to legal complications for both the seller and buyer. Making payments through RTGS or bank draft will help avoid such complications and litigation for both parties.

6. If you are the seller and handing over property documents to the buyer, make sure to keep a color photocopy or scanned copy of all the property papers. This will ensure that you don't face any issues in the future.

7. If you are taking a property loan, make sure to obtain confirmation from the bank that they have received all the required documents from you as per their requirements.

Precautions while selling your property

1. The first precaution is that until the property registration is complete, you should not hand over the original documents to anyone. Many people create scanned copies of property documents and share them. However, misuse of scanned copies could lead to the creation of fake documents, so you should never share scanned color copies with anyone. If a buyer or broker asks for the original documents, you can show original documents and take documents back. You can provide black and white photocopies of the documents for verification purposes, and if you wish, you can put a cross mark on these copies to prevent any misuse. But remember, you should not provide the original documents until the registration is finalized.

2. You should never give possession of the property to the buyer before the registry. Under no circumstances should you hand over the keys of your

house or shop to the buyer before the registry, even if they insist on it.

3. If your property is rented out, mention in the agreement that your property is under a rental arrangement and that a tenant is currently occupying the house. Also, write in agreement that a copy of the rent agreement has been provided to the buyer. This is important because if you sell the property and the buyer goes to take possession but the tenant refuses to vacate, the buyer might take legal action against you, claiming that he is suffering because of you. Therefore, if your property is rented, include these details in the agreement to inform the buyer that the property was already rented. Ideally, it's best to sell the property after vacating the tenant.

4. When a buyer purchases a property using a loan, there is often a clause that if the buyer's loan application is not approved, the agreement will be cancelled. While this clause provides a safety net for the buyer, it can be problematic for the seller. In such cases, the seller's time is wasted, and any money received as part of the agreement might need to be returned to the buyer. Two common scenarios result in loan disapproval: either the buyer is ineligible for the loan due to factors such as less than desired loan eligibility or there are issues with the property itself, such as title problems. To address this, the seller can add a clause stating that if the loan application is rejected due to property-related issues, only then will the agreement be canceled. Meanwhile, the buyer should ensure that their loan is pre-sanctioned to avoid any complications arising from loan eligibility or credit score issues. This provides a more balanced approach, safeguarding both the buyer's and seller's interests.

5. Whenever you sell a property, make sure to keep a copy of the new registry for your records. Also, advise the buyer to update the property's entry in the municipality records. Often, buyers forget to update the property's entry, leading to situations where house tax or water tax continues to be billed in the seller's name.

6. On the day of registration, when you hand over the property documents to the buyer, create a list of the property documents on a separate sheet of paper and have the buyer sign the list as a form of acknowledgment.

7. If you are selling a joint property, the funds from the buyer should be deposited into each owner's respective accounts. For instance, if two brothers share a property 50-50, the money should be divided into their accounts in a 50-50 ratio. Avoid the situation where you take the entire amount into your account and giving your brother's share in cash, doing

illegal cash transaction while retaining the white component for yourself. Such actions could lead your brother to claim in the future that he did not receive his rightful share of the money.

Precautions while dealing with property dealers

1. If you are a seller and you have hired a broker who will show your property to potential buyers and take a certain percentage, it is advisable to create a simple agreement with the broker outlining the terms and conditions. For example, specify the percentage of brokerage the broker will charge, the timing for collecting the brokerage, the broker's responsibilities, and your responsibilities as a seller. You can include copies of the broker's PAN card and Aadhar card in the agreement and have them signed by two witnesses. By doing all this, you will legally engage the broker and the broker will also have responsibilities.

2. Generally, RERA (Real Estate Regulatory Authority) approved brokers are more reliable compared to non-RERA approved brokers. So, if you have two options, it's advisable to choose the RERA approved broker.

3. Under no circumstances, you should hand over the original documents of your property to the broker. If the broker wishes to see the original documents, you can take the documents to show them, but you should not give the documents to the broker. If the broker requests photocopies, you should provide them in black and white with a crossed-out mark, ensuring that your property papers cannot be misused.

4. If a broker asks you for keys to show the flat or house to potential buyers, try to avoid giving the keys to the broker if possible. You can give the keys to a trusted neighbor or friend to show the property. If it's necessary to give the keys to the broker, use a lock that requires two keys—one in your possession and the other with the broker. Avoid using a Lock that can be changed easily. If feasible, provide a key for a specific door lock that cannot be easily changed.

5. Never create a General Power of Attorney (GPA) in the broker's name. Avoid generating any document that grants the broker the right to sell or gift the property on your behalf.

6. Never sign on any blank agreement at the broker's office under any circumstances.

7. Whenever you visit a broker, they might tell you that the prevailing rate in a certain area is a particular amount. Never rely solely on a single broker when dealing with property matters. If you go to a broker to sell a property, they might quote a lower rate, saying that selling the property is

very difficult and you won't get a better price. On the other hand, if you're interested in buying a property, the broker might claim that the rates have significantly increased and will continue to rise, pressuring you to make a quick decision. To determine the correct property rate, it's advisable to confirm the rates from multiple brokers in that area.

8. Whenever you pay brokerage, make sure to do so through online transactions. Avoid giving cash to the broker. This has the advantage that if any dispute arises, you can provide proof of the broker's involvement.

9. If a property broker suggests that they will bring the agreement for the buyer to sign, avoid agreeing to this immediately. Instead, ensure that the buyer signs the agreement in your presence and ask the buyer to bring their Aadhar and PAN card. By doing this, you can protect yourself from potential fraud.

10. In today's time, online fraud is also prevalent. For example, fake brokers on online portals might take token amounts into their accounts and then disappear. Note:Despite conducting thorough due diligence, there can still be instances of fraud or unexpected outcomes in property transactions same as in marriage, delivery of baby or undergoing surgery, risk is inherent in various aspects of life. Even medical treatments involve risks but people still opt for surgeries to resolve health issues. Similarly, when you buy property, there's always an element of risk. However, with careful research, diligence and thoughtful decision-making, you can mitigate the risks associated with property purchases.

Benifits of Leave & License Agreement while renting your property

If you want to rent out your house or flat to a tenant, you can create a leave and license agreement instead of a rent agreement. In this article, I will explain the benefits of a leave and license agreement.

1. When you give a property on a leave and license agreement, the tenant or licensee does not receive the property's interest or legal possession. They are granted the right to use the property under certain conditions. On the other hand, if you rent out the property, the tenant gets legal possession and interest in the property. For instance, a tenant can get utility connections like electricity, water, and internet in their name, but a licensee cannot do so. When you sign a rent agreement or lease deed, you legally and technically transfer physical possession to the tenant. In contrast, when you sign a leave and license agreement, you grant the tenant the right to use the property, providing them with a form of physical possession, while retaining legal and technical possession yourself.

2. In the case of a rental agreement, you can only ask the tenant to vacate the property when there is a violation of certain conditions or when the agreement expires. Evicting a tenant from a property can be quite challenging due to laws that often favor tenants. On the other hand, in a leave and license agreement, it is generally easier to get the property vacated.

3. When you sign a rent agreement or lease deed, tenant laws such as rent control Acts can be enforced, which often favor the tenant and can lead to lengthy legal battles. In contrast, when you sign a leave and license agreement, the tenant cannot enforce rent control Acts against you. In such cases, as a landlord, you can avoid various legal disputes.

4. In the case of a leave and license agreement, if the licensor (landlord) or licensee (tenant) passes away, the agreement is considered canceled. For instance, if the tenant dies, the agreement is considered void. However, in the case of a rent agreement, the death of the tenant does not result in automatic cancellation, and the legal heirs of the tenant retain their rights to continue residing on the property.

5. If you are selling a property, your rent agreement does not automatically cancel upon selling the property. However, in the case of a leave and license agreement, the agreement is terminated on selling the property.

6. If you have created a rent agreement, the tenant can sublease your property unless your rental agreement explicitly prohibits subleasing. On the other hand, if you create a leave and license agreement, the tenant or licensee cannot sublease your property.

7. A Leave and License Agreement and a Rent Agreement are practically similar, but creating a Leave and License Agreement enhances the legal rights of the landlords. In case of legal disputes, having a Leave and License Agreement makes it easier for the landlord to resolve the issues and reclaim the property.

8. To create a Leave and License Agreement, you'll need to make some changes to a typical Rent Agreement. Instead of "landlord," you have to use "licensor," and instead of "tenant," you have to use "licensee." "Rent" will become "license fee," and "rental agreement" will become "leave and license agreement." While renting out a house, you provide keys to the tenant, but in the legal terms of a Leave and License Agreement the property's exclusive possession is not with the licensee. If you want to make a Leave and License Agreement, you can seek assistance from a lawyer.

9. If possible try to register leave and license agreement. You have to pay registration fee but your legal right will be increase as landlord.

Note: These advice or precautions and tips a`are not legal advice and I do not claim that this article is completely true or authentic. Please consult your lawyer for taking any decision regarding property purchase

CHAPTER XLIX

Capital gain

In simple terms whenever anyone is selling capital asset and get some profit or gains in selling process, it is considered as capital gain. In general,land, house, office or commercial space is considered as a capital asset.

There are two types of capital gains.

(i) Short term capital gain (ii) long term capital gain

Particular	Long term capital gain	Short term capital gain
Period	Property sold after 2 years from purchase date	Property sold within 2 years from purchase date
Indexation	Yes	No
Tax rate	20%	30%
Exemption Tax saving	Yes	No
Section in which tax saving can be done	54,54EC,54F	No

Types of capital gains

<u>Section 54</u>

- Only Individuals or Hindu Undivided Families (HUFs) can claim this exemption.
- The **asset being sold** should be a **Residential House**.
- The **taxpayer must invest the Capital Gains by purchasing a residential house** either 1 year before the date of sale or 2 years after the date of sale. In case the seller is constructing a house, the seller will have to construct the residential house within 3 years from the date of sale and hold new purchased residential property for 3 years.
- Note: From 1st April 2023 the capital gains tax exemption under **Section 54 is restricted to Rs.10 crore**. Earlier, there was no threshold.
- Note: With effect from Assessment Year 2020-21 corresponding to FY 2019-20, a capital gain exemption is available for purchase of two residential houses in India. However, the exemption is subject to the capital gain not exceeding Rs 2 crore. Also, the exemption is available only once in the lifetime of the seller.

Section 54F

- Only Individuals or Hindu Undivided Families (HUFs) can claim this exemption.
- The **asset being sold** should be any **long-term capital asset, not being a residential house.**
- The taxpayer should **invest the complete sales amount** of the long-term capital asset in purchase of a new residential house.
- The **new residential property must be purchased** either 1 year before or 2 years after the sale of asset or constructed within 3 years of sale of old asset and hold new purchased residential property for 3 years.
- **Taxpayer should not own more than one residential house on the date of sale**, other than the one bought for claiming exemption under this section.
- Note: From 1ˢᵗ April 2023 the capital gains tax exemption under **Section 54F is restricted to Rs.10 crore**. Earlier, there was no threshold.

Section 54EC

- **Any taxpayer can claim** this exemption.
- The **asset being sold should be a Long Term Capital Asset,** which includes land or building or mutual funds or stocks.
- The taxpayer must **invest the Capital Gains within 6 months** from the date of transfer.
- The **investment should be made in 54EC bonds** for example National Highways Authority of India (NHAI), Rural Electrification Corporation (REC), Power Finance Corporation Limited (PFC) bonds, or Indian Railway Finance Corporation (IRFC) Limited bonds and minimum holding time for investing in bonds will be 5 years.
- The **total investment cannot exceed INR 50 lakhs.**

Particular	Section 54	Section 54F	Section 54EC
Who can claim	Individual or HUF	Anyone	Individual or HUF
Asset being sold	Residential house	Any long-term capital asset, not being a residential house.	Any Long Term Capital Asset (Note: Taxpayer should not own more than one residential house on the date of sale)
How much investment	Only Long Term Capital Gain amount	Complete sales amount	Only Long Term Capital Gain amount
When and where to invest	Residential house	Residential house	54EC Bonds
Time limit for new investment	Purchase :1 year backward or 2 year forward. Construction: 3 years forward	Purchase :1 year backward or 2 year forward. Construction: 3 years forward	Within 6 months
Exemption amount	Investment in the new asset or capital gain,whichever is lower(max Rs.10Cr)	(Long Term capital gain*amount invested in new house)divided by Sale proceeds of original assets (max Rs.10Cr)	Investment in the new asset or capital gain,whichever is lower(max Rs.50lakhs)

Capital gain Exepmtions